D0934240

# JOCK
# CULTURE
# U.S.A.

BY THE SAME AUTHOR

Checking Back: The Story of NHL Hockey

GV
706.5
.I82
1978

# JOCK
# CULTURE
# U.S.A.

## NEIL D. ISAACS

W·W· NORTON & COMPANY, INC. NEW YORK

INDIANA
PURDUE
LIBRARY
MAR 6 1979

FORT WAYNE

Grateful acknowledgment is made to Farrar, Straus & Giroux, Inc., for permission to reprint "Say Good-bye to Big Daddy," from *The Complete Poems* by Randall Jarrell, copyright © 1966 by Mrs. Randall Jarrell; to Quadrangle/The New York Times Book Co., for permission to reprint excerpts from Robert Lipsyte's *Sports-World*, copyright © 1975 by Robert Lipsyte; to Houghton Mifflin Company for permission to reprint excerpts from Don DeLillo's *End Zone*, copyright © 1972 by Don DeLillo; to Alfred A. Knopf, Inc., for permission to reprint excerpts from *Rabbit, Run*, copyright © 1960 by John Updike, and *Rabbit Redux*, copyright © 1971 by John Updike. Quotations from "Princeton," *The Great Gatsby*, and *This Side of Paradise* by F. Scott Fitzgerald are reprinted by permission of Charles Scribner's Sons and are fully protected by copyright.

Copyright © 1978 by Neil D. Isaacs
Published simultaneously in Canada by George J. McLeod Limited, Toronto.
Printed in the United States of America.

All Rights Reserved
First Edition

Library of Congress Cataloging in Publication Data

Isaacs, Neil David, 1931–
Jock culture U.S.A.

1. Sports—Social aspects—United States.
2. Sports—Social aspects. 3. Sports—Philosophy.
I. Title.
GV706.5.I82 1978    796'.01    77–26114
ISBN 0–393–08807–3

Book design by Antonina Krass
Typefaces used are V.I.P. Caledonia and Typositor Stymie Open
Book manufactured by Vail-Ballou Press, Inc.

1 2 3 4 5 6 7 8 9 0

To the memory of
**ANNIE BRAUN,**

whose last words to me
(Neil, you know how much I loved you all)
will stay with me as a benediction all my days,
and to her namesake and great-granddaughter,
who in a single decade has already given
a lifetime of joy to many,
with much love

# CONTENTS

# ACKNOWLEDGMENTS

I am grateful to many people for contributions to this book, but especially to Jack Higgs, who has been a significant influence from its inception.

For the rest I have space only to say thank you and hope I've included everyone in the following list. It includes classroom guests (several of whom have allowed me to quote them in the text), students who shared their insights and deepest convictions with me, people who provided forums for testing some of my ideas, and a variety of other friends, helpers, and informants. Gracias y saludos amigos: Larry Batson, Harold Bell, Bob Berger, Andy Beyer, Dewey Blanton, Alan Bloomingdale, Jack Bryer, Greta Coen, Dick Comer, Dick Darcey, Donald Dell, Bill Deoudes, David DuPree, Bob Edwards, Noel Epstein, Bob Ferry, Tom Fields, Tom Gasque, Larry Harrison, Arnold Heft, Steve Hershey, Bob Hofler, Kim Hoover, John Howard, Mo Howard, Jonny Isaacs, David Israel, Roy Jefferson, Jimmy Jones, Jim Kehoe, Wally Keiderling, Howard Labow, Stan Lavine, Ellen Levine, Don Linehan, John Lucas, Dorothy McKnight, Jack Mann, Patricia Farrell Mayo, Ron Mottl, Peter O'Malley, Abe Pollin, Shirley Povich, Doug Radebaugh,

Frank Romano, Harry Rosenfeld, Kenny Roy, Don Ruck, Jack Russell, Patricia Ryan, Jerry Sachs, Tom Scarbath, John Schultz, R. L. Schwartz, Tom Seppy, Len Shapiro, Dave Sheehan, George Solomon, Eric Stevens, Gerry Strine, Pat Summerall, Eric Swenson, Bill Tanton, Shelby Whitfield, Ted Wright, Jack Zane.

# JOCK
# CULTURE
# U.S.A.

# I

## PRIME TIME

The sports pages may have carried the scores buried somewhere on a back page. You can find them in the soccer magazines and annuals for 1970. They say, simply, that in a preliminary round of the World Cup competition, Honduras defeated El Salvador 1–0 at home, El Salvador defeated Honduras 3–0 at home, and in the deciding match on a neutral field in Mexico El Salvador eliminated Honduras 3–2.

To gain some perspective on what those results meant, you would go on to discover that El Salvador defeated Haiti (which had shut out the United States to get there) in the regional finals. El Salvador won at home 2–1, lost in Haiti 3–0, and won the rubber game on a neutral field in Kingston town 1–0. The Salvadorans thus qualified for the Group 1 round-robin playoffs along with Mexico, Belgium, and the USSR.

In that round the Soviets won with Mexico as runner-up, both moving on to the quarterfinals. Belgium had won just one game, 3–0 against El Salvador. Both the USSR and Mexico were knocked out in the quarters, by Uruguay (which lost to champion Brazil in the semis) and Italy (which lost the championship after beating West Germany 4–3). In other words, among the final six-teen teams at Mexico City, El Salvador couldn't even score against teams that were themselves badly beaten in other world-class com-petition.

No wonder the preliminary results in the Group 13 competi-tion rated so little attention in the sports pages. But you will find quite a different story in the pages of a learned journal called *International Affairs* or the *Strategic Survey 1969* published by the In-stitute for Strategic Studies in London. It goes like this.

The first game was played on June 8, 1969, in Tegucigalpa, Honduras. The Salvadoran team and fans came home complaining they had been mistreated. When the Honduran team arrived for the second game in San Salvador, the players were hounded by angry crowds. After getting beat, Honduran players complained they had not been allowed to sleep.

Hondurans howled outrage at having "their women defiled, their menfolk assaulted and the national flag desecrated." Riots fol-lowed in every main town of Honduras. Shops owned by Sal-vadorans were burned and looted, there were many casualties, including an unspecified number of fatalities. Salvadorans, crying massacre, fled for the home border or for Nicaragua, whichever was closer. El Salvador screamed "genocide" in an official state-ment, mobilized its military reserves, and broke off diplomatic and economic relations.

Nevertheless, the soccer series stood at one game each, and the rubber match was played in Mexico City the following week. Honduras, losing 3–2, failed to save face. While both countries ap-pealed to the OAS for reparations, their armies deployed at the border. Eventually they exchanged fire on the ground and both sides launched air raids (both countries had a handful of Mustangs and Corsairs, World War II American fighters). On July 14, El Sal-vador invaded Honduras, occupying territory until August 5, when the OAS imposed a shaky peace. Perhaps as many as two thousand people had been killed and there were perhaps as many as a hundred thousand refugees, before the threat of severe economic sanctions ended what has come to be called the "Soccer War."

Even in jest—and it would be a joke with cosmic irony—nobody could claim that the sporting event was the reason for the war. Though members of a common market, Honduras and El Salvador are what might be called natural enemies. One is an underdeveloped, sparsely populated country, exporting primarily agricultural products, plagued with chronic unemployment and land-reform problems, and infected with a nationalism and xenophobia by the influential presence of foreign investment; the other is relatively highly developed and industrialized, the most densely populated in the hemisphere (equal to Italy), with a frighteningly high birth rate and considerable social strife fueled by the presence of a small, tightly knit oligarchy. Emigrating Salvadorans made up one eighth of the population of Honduras and an even higher percentage of its work force.

Yet the sporting event gave the war an immediate reason. It is too simple to say that both governments used the incidents surrounding the soccer games as pretexts for political action, for aggressive acts. That much is obvious. The question is how they were able to do it. How did the national soccer teams become embodiments of nationalistic sentiments and in turn symbols of international politico-economic interests? Any adequate answer would have to explain the nature of sport in Latin American cultures, would have to include speculations on the dynamics of machismo in the Latin psyche, and would have to observe the almost simplistic ways in which sports are identified with class and place and race as well as nation. Indeed, it *is* in sporting events, not wars or revolutions, that Latin Americans act out their rituals of identity, distinction, and achievement.

How different this almost primitive picture is from the sophisticated place of Nordamericano sports in our culture. Forget the socio-political gestures on Olympic victory stands in Mexico City. Never mind the Montreal riot when Clarence Campbell suspended Rocket Richard. Set aside the incidental violence and casualties in football and baseball riots in out-of-the-way places like Knoxville, Columbus, Pittsburgh, and New York. Let alone the grim competition for medals between the USSR and the United

States—we wouldn't want to argue that the Games serve to ritualize the cold war by overheated athletic exertions. Surely in the United States we wouldn't be incited to riot or loot or kill by reason of a sporting event. We might go to court, but not to war. In our culture sports have their place, but they are kept in their place, are they not? When sports-consciousness creeps into other aspects of our lives, our language, and other institutions of our society, that's all just metaphor, is it not?

No, they are not. Alas, it is not. Latin American governments recognize the power of sport by having a minister of sport in every cabinet. In the United States, that power is wielded in a number of unofficial, unrecognized, indirect, and insidious ways. That is one major difference between the Latin American scene and ours, and there is another that suggests why I have begun with the Soccer War by way of contrast.

If you read the works of the leading Latin American writers—Amado, Borges, Bioy Casares, Cortázar, Espinal, Fuentes, Garcia Marquez, Juarroz, Moyano, Neruda, Paz, Vallejo, and Vargas-Llosa, to name a few in no special order—and if you experience the artifacts of Latin American cultures—painting, sculpture, film, song—you will find no awareness of sport whatsoever. No soccer, no baseball, no tennis, no track, no golf. As important as sport is in Latin American life, it is all partaken on a surface level of consciousness. It is universally accepted there, and it remains there, never seeping through into the profound levels of artistic expression. Or, to put it another way, sport in Latin America is its own art form, embraced wholeheartedly and kept whole in spirit and body because uncorrupted by and unconfused with other institutions or modes of expression.

It is not so simple as that with us. So sophisticated are we, so thoroughly and subtly has the acceptance and awareness of sport filtered into every aspect of our consciousness, that it is taken for granted. Our culture is saturated with sports-mindedness. Our major writers all treat sports directly or indirectly as a given of our society. Our plastic artifacts and our performing arts dote on them.

Our educational system often seems to use them as its *raison d'être*. In the newspapers, the prominence of sports sections is obvious, but we also find sports prominent in other sections— comics, amusements, gossip, editorial—and even on the front page. Check sometime on how much of the advertising is directly or subtly sports-oriented. The prominence is even more striking on television. Set aside the prime-time sports viewing per se and consider the sports orientation and sports-mindedness of situation comedy, game show, talk show, news show, and advertising.

Sports are not simply the surface rituals for us that our hemispheric neighbors embrace so wholly if not wholesomely. For us, sport has entered the fabric and structure of our whole way of life. Sport is a constant, a model, a value system. It is our strength and our weakness, our redeemer and destroyer (though Shelley would shudder at this application of his words). Intellectually and philosophically, emotionally and psychologically, sexually and physically, sport governs our lives. It is not quite enough to recognize, as Robert Lipsyte has in *SportsWorld,* and Michael Novak in *The Joy of Sports,* and James Michener in *Sports in America* (among many others), the great influence of sports on our systems. We must go further and recognize that our system as a whole has become, that the U.S.A. *is,* a jockocracy.

*Jock Culture, U.S.A.* is a statement of my own recognition of this complex phenomenon. It is an essay that argues a position arrived at with a great deal of self-soul-searching as well as a great deal of attention to what I have seen and heard and read over four decades of sports-fandom. Because, after all, I am a fan, and I continue to support a wide variety of sports, despite a growing awareness of the many evils in the sports world and the graver dangers with which it threatens our society at large. As sports-minded as any, I am concerned for the implications of that mind set. As a critic of sports, I must always be aware of the element of self-analysis in my constructions.

The brief introduction to Lipsyte's *SportsWorld* expresses so nearly the same general premises as my original prospectus for

*Jock Culture, U.S.A.*, even echoing some of its language, that the casual reader might have expected the same book. Indeed, the only other editor besides my present one who read that prospectus rejected the idea with a kind of shock that said "I can't publish this because I'm already publishing this, by Lipsyte."

Now I find a delightful irony in this, because the books are so totally different. Lipsyte's is a memoir-in-pastiche of his own rites of passage as a SportsWorld reporter, columnist, commentator, and critic. His growing awareness, building toward the enlightenment that his Introduction reveals, is an underlying theme of the book, but its substance is still sportswriting with its elevation of events and its deification of participants. What gives weight to his opinions is his intimacy with Mantle, Stengel, Lombardi, Dick Tiger, Bill Bradley, Althea Gibson, and especially Muhammad Ali. And it seems to me important that from his perspective, too, one can arrive at an awareness of the danger that sports values are subverting our institutions:

> The values of the arena and the locker room have been imposed upon our national life. Coaches and sportswriters are speaking for generals and businessmen, too, when they tell us that a man must be physically and psychologically "tough" to succeed, that he must be clean and punctual and honest, that he must bear pain, bad luck, and defeat without whimpering or making excuses. A man must prove his faith in sports and the American Way by whipping himself into shape, playing by the rules, being part of the team, and putting out all the way. If his faith is strong enough, he will triumph. It's his own fault if he loses, fails, remains poor.
>
> Even for ballgames, these values, with their implicit definitions of manhood, courage, and success, are not necessarily in the individual's best interests. But for daily life they tend to create a dangerous and grotesque web of ethics and attitudes, an amorphous infrastructure that acts to contain our energies, divert our passions, and socialize us for work or war or depression.
>
> I call this infrastructure SportsWorld. For most of my adult life, as a professional observer, I've explored SportsWorld and marveled at its incredible power and pervasiveness. SportsWorld touches every-

one and everything. We elect our politicians, judge our children, fight our wars, plan our vacations, oppress our minorities by SportsWorld standards that somehow justify our foulest and freakiest deeds, or at least camouflage them with jargon. We get stoned on such SportsWorld spectaculars as the Super Bowl, the space shots, the Kentucky Derby, the presidential conventions, the Indianapolis 500, all of whose absurd excesses reassure us that we're okay.

SportsWorld is a sweaty Oz you'll never find in a geography book, but since the end of the Civil War it has been promoted and sold to us like Rancho real estate, an ultimate sanctuary, a university for the body, a community for the spirit, a place to hide that glows with that time of innocence when we believed that rules and boundaries were honored, that good triumphed over evil, and that the loose ends of experience could be caught and bound and delivered in an explanation as final and as comforting as a goodnight kiss.

Sometime in the last fifty years the sports experience was perverted into a SportsWorld state of mind in which the winner was good because he won; the loser, if not actually bad, was at least reduced, and had to prove himself over again, through competition.

Like Lipsyte's, this book records a learning experience. I am glad that I have been able to go on learning—often through teaching. When I initiated my course, "Sports Culture, USA," at the University of Maryland in the spring of 1975, it was with an excitement that I hadn't experienced since my first "film as literature" course back in 1970 at The University of Tennessee. The response of my students fueled my enthusiasm (and renewed the course for subsequent semesters), and I am grateful to them. The structure of the course allowed me to learn much more from my guests than any formal course of study I might have undertaken myself. The following pages will refer frequently to those guests, though probably not to the extent that their influence merits.

It was with due deliberation that I described and designed "Sports Culture, USA" as an attempt to raise the consciousness of as many people as possible (including myself) about the enormous influence of sports on the values, the structures, the institutions, and the artifacts of our culture. The journals of my students testify to a certain measure of success in that design, and in a way this book is the measure of my success in raising my own consciousness.

I discovered that *sports* was the magic word. More people are drawn to a course by that word than by such other mesmerizing mantras as *sex, love, myth, death, money, violence, black, fantasy, women, ecology,* and *city.* The PR machine begins to grind, and the media begin to pay attention. People heard my name and saw pictures of me and talked about what I was doing as if I were someone new. Over a hundred items in my bibliography, including eight books, had never aroused anyone's interest outside a narrow academic, disciplinary context. Now a short interview with Bob Edwards on National Public Radio's "All Things Considered" brought me letters from all over the country. Because I was "doing" sports, I was suddenly somebody. Maybe I could have been a contender.

No object lesson could have been plainer than this. And it was reinforced by the willingness, even eagerness, of prominent people to visit my classroom and talk sports from their special vantage points. The assigned literature, which I still regard as a significant record of the wholesale embracing of sports by our culture (and vice versa), became less a focus and more peripheral to what we were doing in the course. Even in a structured critique of sports, sport was co-opting the action and the approach. Parts of this book, I trust, will restore the proper perspective.

The ongoing experience of the course has given me more than mere enthusiasm and more than a body of original material from the various expertise of my guests. It has given me a way of structuring this essay. By forcing me to isolate and organize the issues, the course has provided me with a logical sequence of ideas. The seven chapters that follow this introduction are the orderly product of what began as an open-ended, free-wheeling, even chaotic investigation. It had premises but no preconceived conclusions and no formalized way to get at conclusions anyway.

One of the broadest issues, encountered in discussions of virtually ever other issue, is the question of heroes. Whether we talk about mythology or history or contemporary fields of activity or fiction, we meet figures larger than life who embody admirable qualities and perform memorable feats. The chapter called "Of Finer Stuff" attempts to examine the heroic nature as our society presently perceives it, but placing that perception in a larger, traditional context. What emerges is a set of conditions under which heroes are found in our society *only* in sports, where charismatic qualities are felt, nourished, projected, and protected.

Only sports support the notion of a separate, sacrosanct world, which seems universally to be necessary for producing and sustaining the heroic image. It is that kind of special world where ritual scenarios are acted out, where mythic narratives are celebrated. The media help to construct that world, to maintain its illusions of specialness, and to create our heroes.

The media are the contemporary vehicles of myth, and the way they handle sports reporting seems in effect to be designed for the cultivation of heroes. By using the performances, especially the records, as their substance, they elevate athletic results to the level of heroic feats. Then, because heroes must *be* heroic, must have heroic qualities, as well as do heroic things, the media create this dimension through their image-making function or power. But even where media fail actively to complete the heroic image, a charismatic athlete may excite the creative imagination of the public to adorn a performer of deeds with excellences of character.

The interrelationship of sports and the arts in our society is thus introduced. "The Laurel and the Ivy" discusses the reflection of sports-mindedness in the arts, with emphasis on literature. A brief overview of the contemporary scene, ranging from "serious" literature to mass media, demonstrates how thoroughly we have embraced and taken for granted the significance of sports. Only ancient Greece, in Western civilization, approaches our universal acceptance of athletic importance.

An important influence on this chapter is Robert J. Higgs,

whose doctoral dissertation was "The Athlete Hero in American Literature." A friend, former student, and now teacher, Jack Higgs is my collaborator in editing *The Sporting Spirit: Athletes in Literature and Life* (originally called *Apollo Agonistes* until the publishers chose to sacrifice sense and taste to an assumption about sales), an anthology for textbook use. One aspect of this subject to which I draw special attention is the way recent American fiction has cast and recast a mythology of football, from a phase of hero worship with its own dark side, through a phase of debunking, to a remythologizing phase.

I also draw attention to the phenomenon of artists going out of their way to cultivate personal associations with athletes. This is also increasingly true of others, like politicians and entertainers, as the celebrity syndrome and the phenomenon of "media personalities" tend to cluster around the sports world. Thus the appropriateness of the next chapter title, "Ten Cents a Dance." Written by Rodgers and Hart for the 1930 Ed Wynn vehicle, *Simple Simon*, and made popular by Ruth Etting's inimitable performance, the song refers primarily to the hard road of a dance-hall hostess but in a larger sense to the universal selling of talent for the pleasure of others.

Sports have been carried so far beyond mythic and ritualistic roles in our society that we must question what their roles and functions are. Ever-increasing leisure time in a capitalistic system has promoted a huge industry of leisure. Play is a serious, practical thing, and sports are big business. But what kind of business is it? Where can a line be drawn between pure entertainment and prostitution? The role of participation sports in filling leisure time vacuums will be discussed in a later chapter. The issue here is the place of sports in the entertainment business at large.

Beyond the filling of leisure time, sports have civilizing functions in a complex, pluralistic society. In general, sports serve the political function of maintaining the order of the status quo, which may be why so many sports institutions and officials are conservative and authoritarian. "The athletic establishment" is not merely a metaphorical phrase. Threats to law and order, the peaceful continuation of things-as-they-are (however repressive), are dispersed by providing the distractions of multiple and highly organized and persistently publicized sports.

Threats to morale in the perceptions of class, privilege, discrimination, power imbalance, and the like are diffused by providing healthy competition, avenues for releasing aggression, channels for legitimizing (and displacing) the bitterness and envy produced by real or imagined injustices. At a summer camp, the symbolic hostility of the traditional "color war" is designed to produce healthy integration and unity and allegiance. In Latin America, where sports are always given top priority by military dictatorships, nothing pleases, say, a Dominican regime more or is a better guarantee of domestic tranquillity than to have every able-bodied cane-working Domenicano playing the *besbol* (organized or pickup) with whatever energy he has left after a day in the fields.

But sports can also provide a vehicle for social change. In our society we can see that the causes of minorities and women have been advanced through athletics. The movements toward racial and sexual equality in sports are given primary attention in this discussion, supported by interviews with Roy Jefferson, David DuPree, and Dorothy McKnight. A focal issue here is whether athletic establishments coopt the instrumentality for change either by giving the false illusion of a genuine progressive impulse or by holding out false hopes for the many in the token acceptance of the few.

At the heart of the book is a chapter called "Withered Garlands," which deals with the question of values in a sports-minded society. Sports, through the myth-making process, may reflect society's values, but through the socializing process may also instruct and inculcate values. Thus there is a danger that values may be subverted, and we must search out the means of measuring that danger by finding the signs of subversion.

The clearest signs are subtle and slow to emerge, but they may be seen in the shifting of priorities. The values of the game become subordinated to the values of winning. The system or organization takes precedence over the things systematized and organized; the reasons for system or organization in the first place are subordinated to reasons for maintaining the system or organization. Little League baseball (like major league baseball itself) loses sight of its purpose—to provide structures for the game of baseball to be played and enjoyed by all—and becomes jealous of its power and structure, acquiring new purposes along the way: to win, without regard to the players; to exclude those who may intrude "irrelevant" or "upsetting" elements; to allow adults to play out fantasy roles of management and authority in competition.

When the supreme values of winning are combined with an ultimate profit motive, sports become powerful, living texts for an ends-justify-means philosophy. Sport, then, reinforces or even develops shortsighted value judgments in the military, economic, political, judicial, and ethical systems of our society.

In individual, psychological terms, too, the transvaluations may obtain. The positive values of team play and ego satisfaction may give way to a kind of jingoistic violence and to all sorts of aggressive behavior. Instead of dissipating destructive forces, sports may breed them. And the confusion of gain on levels of individual and group achievement can produce dysfunctions of both game and system, both team and player alike.

Moreover, when sports most openly preach positive values, they may show these most clearly in practice to be cosmetic coverings for aggressive drives. A case in point is the famous "Pyramid of Success," taken by many as the symbol not only of John Wooden's unprecedented record as a college basketball coach but also as a tribute to the character of the man as elder statesman and sporting philosopher. An examination of the copyrighted pyramid, however, in the context of the personality that erected it and the application of it to actual practice, reveals it as a monument to pious hypocrisy—another commonplace of Jock Culture, U.S.A.

The conservative tendency of sports structures not to

change, even in the face of changing external conditions, may be self-destructive. A discussion of Robert Coover's *Universal Baseball Association, J. Henry Waugh, Prop.* is appropriate here, along with some of the anomalies in athletics as catalogued by such writers as Jack Scott, Harry Edwards, and George Leonard. On the other hand, radical changes in sports structures may be equally destructive, as dramatized in such films as *Roller Ball* and *Death Race 2,000* and such phenomena as the wholesale proliferation of professional leagues.

Finally, this chapter will discuss a curious product of our society's conditioning to the absolute value of winning. The grand, rosy hopes that were summed up in Charles Reich's phrase, "the greening of America," have gone aglimmering in what I call "the graying of the greening." I attribute the failure of the counterculture to its inability to overcome that conditioning. Once the name of *losers* was identified with and accepted by and for those with alternative ways for a better future, their causes were lost as well.

For one of the most intriguing confusions of values in our society, I have reserved a separate chapter. It is the hypocritical proscription of gambling, an activity universally associated with if not an integral part of athletic competition. "Action and the Puritan Ethic" will examine the problem briefly in the context of this book's focus, but I must reserve for a future book a far more extensive cultural-historical treatment of the subject.

Among my sources for this chapter are interviews with Gerald Strine of the *Washington Post* and Andrew Beyer of the *Washington Star*, a statement from an articulate bookmaker who will have to remain anonymous, and material from the Commission on the Review of the National Policy toward Gambling and the House Select Committee on Professional Sports. From them, from an army of secondhand sources, and from common and personal knowledge, a clear picture emerges: if sport is big business, sports betting is a giant conglomerate; if sports are corrupt, they are corrupt whether or not there is gambling associated with them and whether or not the gambling is legal; and if there is a strong desire to keep sport honest, nowhere is that desire more pronounced and important than among those who make bets and make book on sporting events.

Chapter VII is called "The Contagion of Competition" and moves into a general discussion of the subversion of other institutions by sports-mindedness and sports values. The discussion may be somewhat fragmented because I try to touch briefly on as many areas as possible. Our political system comes most readily to mind ("fandom rampant on a public field"), with all its jingoism and gut-level chauvinism. The structure of our political processes comes more and more to resemble athletic formats, and the recent proposal for "regional primaries" in presidential campaigns is a new indication of that process, after the model of the NCAA basketball tournament or the NFL playoff structure. In organizational terms, the model makes good sense, but in effect the danger is that the political process becomes just another social activity removed from reality into an area of ceremonial or ritualistic participation.

Less obvious are connections I would make among religion, sports, and sex. The cultic phenomena of religious revivals seem themselves sportslike, and the connection is strengthened by institutions like the Ys and the Fellowship of Christian Athletes, by traditions like the pregame invocation-cum-anthem, and by events like a Sunday-morning prayer brunch for famous athletes at the White House.

It is in this chapter that I discuss the new emphasis on athletic participation for all. We have developed, under the good auspices of our most influential leaders, and with the best will in the world, a cult of physical well-being. And at its extreme, or extremities, is the worship of sex for itself. This supreme manifestation is typified in the term "sportfucking," and the cult's activities are celebrated with the trappings of sport, including leagues, circuits, arenas, team activities, and an amazing amassing of statistics.

The sporting predilection for statistical records carries over into the most outrageous and obscene areas. Airplane crashes are reported in terms of "worst disaster on a Friday in South Dakota." An earthquake in Guatemala is measured incidentally on a Richter scale; the important scale is the statistics of fatalities: "more than . . . killed, more than . . . homeless—the worst natural disaster in Central American history." Hurricanes are measured not only in the force of the winds by miles per hour but also in the killed, missing, and homeless and perhaps most importantly in dollars' worth of damage. Or a deranged student sets a record for mass killings in Austin, Texas. The headline in the *Washington Post* for July 18, 1966, read, "SNIPER AT TEXAS UNIVERSITY KILLS 15, WOUNDS 32." The first three paragraphs of the story are worth quoting in full:

> A former Marine and honor student killed his wife and mother in the dead of night. He stationed himself atop a University Tower and shot to death 13 other persons before police killed him.
>
> At least 32 other persons were wounded as the sniper crouching on an observation ledge far above the crowded campus sprayed those below him with bullets for 80 minutes.
>
> The sniper, Charles J. Whitman, 24, an architecture honor student from Lake Worth, Fla. surpassed the worst previous mass murder in recent U.S. history—the slaying of 13 persons in Camden, N.J. by berserk World War II veteran Howard Unruh in 1949.

In a follow-up story on August 3, the *Post* repeated the phrase "greatest mass murder in American history" and quoted a psychiatrist who said that Whitman looked like "the All-American boy." All this seems to me a subversion of values.

Passing mention will be made of relationships between sports and several other institutions: the press, medicine, the law, government, and labor. In each case some expert testimony will be called to witness. But I must reserve for a final chapter, "The Graves of Academe," the question of the role and function of sports in the university.

In developing the complete person, the university must obviously find it appropriate to devote some attention to the body. It seems also appropriate to provide the socializing role of group-identification both in actual participation in team sports and in surrogate enjoyment of representative teams. Moreover, the commitment to realizing the full potential of each individual necessarily includes providing facilities for athletic activity. And finally, since sports are an important aspect of our society, it is appropriate for universities to pay some curricular attention to an understanding of sports, their meaning, their function, their history, and their relationships with other disciplines.

But what happens to the idea of a university when an athletic department becomes not only central but powerful and even autonomous? What happens when the ritual functions are confused with profit motives? What happens when the athletic activities of a few are given priority over the athletic activities of most? In the context of a university, I submit that the equation, to try to win = to show a profit, is false and irrelevant.

I argue finally that the question of values in education must be loudly asked when sports are threatening to subvert them. Ideally, education should free the mind and spirit, not bind them and the individual to the job of his choice. The trade-school concept of higher education is taught and reinforced by the sports establishment with its almost absolute quantification of values. This quantifying philosophy is, or should be, anathema to the university, but more and more it comes to control it.

My definition of a public institution of higher education is this: a community of scholars, where the pursuits of knowledge, humane understanding, and critical judgment are *ends in themselves;* where intellectual freedom is *absolute;* and where a pluralistic society can reflect the ideal of learning to live with all possible deviations from the norm without loss of integrity. I submit that the presence of sports is not inconsistent with such a definition, but that overemphasis on the wrong aspects of sports corrupts the processes and the very nature of the university.

# II

# OF FINER STUFF

An official fiction, or myth, that has had great currency for about two centuries goes like this: all men are created equal. Yet mankind's universal perception is that some are more equal than others. Some persons are born with or destined to special power— generally defined as wealth, beauty and strength, or knowledge. In another context, these can become gifts to be resisted, temptations: the world, the flesh, and the devil. But the gifted ones, the power-persons, are everywhere and in all times celebrated as heroes.

The hero may be the cultural invention of his society; that is, his identity or special nature may itself be an official fiction. He may, of course, have earned that identity by his genuine nature or by his accomplishments. The universal presence of such figures in all societies, however, suggests that if we didn't have heroes we'd invent them, that when we don't have heroes we do invent them. I don't mean to insist that the universality proves need. I'm quite willing to entertain the notion that humanity may evolve—may already be evolving—past the process of concretizing concepts in heroic mythic figures. Indeed, the development of abstract symbolism in some art forms in some cultures supports such a notion. But so far we are talking about minority trends. The abstract logo is a long way from replacing the flesh-and-blood (whether real or fictive) personification. A stylized NBC sign is a dwarf in the land of Jolly Green Giants.

Our society in general finds its heroes only in sports. It may be objected that the names of athletes rarely appear on "most admired" lists compiled by public opinion polls. But to extrapolate from the roster of most-admireds to a popular conception of hero would be to stumble into the kind of semantic boobytraps for which pollsters are famous. Only the most abandoned boobies or the more eccentric savants would not respond to the keyword "admired" by searching their frames of reference for people who have been of great service to mankind, either by making real contributions or by enacting symbolic roles of nobility, or people who have won Nobel Prizes, usually for Peace or for Medicine. Admired are the Albert Schweitzers, the Eleanor Roosevelts, the Golda Meirs, the Ralph Bunches, the Jonas Salks. But these are not names that would occur in response to the question, "Who are your heroes?"

*Hero*, like so many other words that embody the great ideas of our culture, comes from the Greek, where it had two nearly distinct meanings. It referred simply to any warrior actively involved in serving the state, or it referred posthumously to a person whose storied accomplishments were celebrated by elevating him to the status of demigod. The latter sense became diffused in many semantic byways and tributaries, while the former has become transformed in the mainstream to the performer of feats more often athletic than not.

When the question *is* asked it is interesting that some answers come from the world of fiction, in this way retaining an aspect of that second Greek sense. Other answers imply the association of idols or models with heroes, apparently unrelated to the Greek meanings, unless we acknowledge the role of mass media in creating and perpetuating the mythic and the legendary. But many answers focus on those athletic warriors actively involved in serving the public by dominating the games they play. Thus a contemporary list might include Superman and Wonder Woman, Jesus and Einstein, Groucho Marx and Evel Knievel, Billie Jean King and Muhammad Ali. Indeed, a poll taken among entering freshmen at Brown University had these very names heading the list last year.

In order to understand how we have arrived at this apparent devaluing of the hero, we must step back a bit and examine from a broad perspective how societies locate their heroes. We have to think about the conditions under which heroic images appear and are projected to a public. Then we have to consider the dual nature of heroes—figures who *are* and *do*, what kinds of perceptions they celebrate, and finally how they may be used. Perhaps we can then arrive at an explanation of why in a crowded movie theater showing *The Towering Inferno,* when the impressive list of stars in a who's who of a cast appears on the screen, the only name to draw cheers is that of O. J. Simpson.

Heroic figures must have vehicles for their image to be communicated. From another point of view, people must have vehicles ' for the recording and celebration of perceptions that seem significant to them. Serving these purposes are the dramatic/narrative structures of ritual and mythology. Without these structures heroes could neither exist nor be perceived as such, and it doesn't make a particle of difference to the heroic nature or function whether the stories told or the acts ceremonially performed represent the "truth" of historical fact. In these terms, official fictions are equal to recorded observations of reality, and symbolic gestures are equal to imitations of observed events. History and fiction are interchangeable for the narrative structures of mythology. And, of course, these structures operate outside of normal profane time and space in a sacrosanct world.

The more important the hero, the more clearly he will be seen to embody a major perception or personalize a major accomplishment of a people. It is not difficult to categorize heroic narratives by a simple distinction: either they celebrate "things as they are and have always been" (perhaps "things as they have been

since the beginning when they came to be this way") or they celebrate "things as they are becoming by means of change." On the
one hand—stasis, a sense of permanence, a belief in eternity and
immutable nature and order; on the other—process, a sense of
transience, an awareness of mortality and mutability and disorder.
This basic dichotomy helps to explain, among other things, why
heroes are most often seen as in conflict, sometimes with each
other, reflections of a perception of polarization. For it is quite
precisely in terms of polarities that most of us perceive the nature
of things.

Take a random sampling of mythic heroes from the various
traditions that make up what we call Western civilization—
Prometheus, Odysseus, Aeneas, Gawain, Beowulf, Odin, Loki.
In every case the stories told about these figures deal with
at least one aspect of the basic polarity—the heroic bringing of a
primordial gift to mankind like fire or language, the heroic defending of an age-old order under attack, the heroic founding of a new
order for the birth or rebirth of an age. A random list of heroic figures drawn from historic personages would serve the same
exemplary purposes—Henry V, George Washington, Martin
Fierro, Alfred the Great, Charlemagne, Saint Patrick.

Now if it is possible briefly to examine any particular hero
character outside the context of his narrative or legend, another
generalization emerges. Heroes always personify qualities that are
admired by or significant to their societies. In such a laboratory
procedure, the findings could argue that these figures are considered heroic because they have the qualities or that they are made
heroic by having the qualities bestowed upon them. In other
words, a hero is a hero because of what he is—Aeneas because of
his goodness, Washington because of his integrity, and the like.

When the character is put back into the context of his scenario, however, an entirely different conclusion may be reached.
The figures seem to be heroic because of the feats they have performed or they are made heroic by "remembering" what they have
accomplished. In other words, a hero is a hero because of what he

does—Beowulf because he fights monsters with the strength of thirty men, Saint Patrick because he frees a land from a plague of monsters, and the like.

A reasonable conclusion that may be drawn from these observations is that heroes both personify qualities that are admired and perform feats that are memorable. If the one is "real," the other may be an official fiction. No wonder, then, that our society looks in vain for heroes outside sports. Where feats are performed, qualities are lacking; where we find qualities, we are likely to find lack of action. We have lost the capacity to accept official fictions about politicians, servicemen, law enforcement people, professional people, artists, etc.; and we have lost the willingness if not the ability to create heroic fictions in public imaginations, however needful of those heroes we may be.

Reviewing Paul Zweig's book, *The Adventurer: The Fate of Adventure in the Western World,* in *The New Yorker* George Steiner wondered at the fact that the astronauts never maintained or even achieved the heroic image that their feats deserved:

> that so enormous a gesture, and one so crowded with the genius of danger heroically mastered, should have proved so ephemeral, should have evoked so little response in the arts, in the general climate of feeling, is a profoundly engrossing, perhaps scandalous fact. It suggests fundamental changes in our very sense of what constitutes adventure, of what there is in mortal enterprise to justify the spell, the lasting innocence, of myth.

Among factors contributing to the "rapid disenchantment with what was unquestionably the quintessential adventure, a prowess of human intelligence, discipline, sheer physical splendor beyond anything but dreams" Steiner proposed "the very perfection of mechanical device, the long-studied calm of machine and man, of man almost machined" that "undermined that sense of risk, of personal terror and identification, which makes experience memorable." This is not quite on the mark, but at least hints at the problem—the image of the astronaut projected to the public was worlds apart from possessing any of the qualities considered heroic in the immediate cultural context. NASA's calculations were incredibly precise in technological terms, incredibly stupid or perverse in human (not to mention humanistic) perceptions. Unless, that is, they were cannily fearful of political potentialities.

In a more important way Steiner was off target. By "little response in the arts" he meant the "high arts," and this is a mistake of enormous proportions if one is concerned with a "general climate of feeling." Thomas Pynchon's "Raketemensch" in *Gravity's Rainbow* can be seen as a unique figure only if one separates the myth-making role of serious fiction from the overwhelmingly dominant contemporary world of popular culture. And in this world Bernie Taupin's and Elton John's "Rocket Man" made effective use of language, image, and metaphor from an extraordinarily abundant context of space mythology.

Space fiction—in books, film, radio programs, TV programs, comic books, comic strips—has been a staple of heroic narrative for at least half a century. The trouble with the astronauts is that they failed to match the popular image of Buck Rogers, Captain Kirk, or Paul Muad Dib (or even Charles Lindbergh as he was popularly conceived). If Steiner wants to see what really happened in the appeal of the arts to a general climate of feelings about the astronauts, he should watch TV and its ratings. He should watch "The Six Million Dollar Man" and—a spinoff which is almost Biblical in its recapitulation of the Adam's rib myth—"The Bionic Woman."

In order to render the astronaut figure as an image of heroism for contemporary society, a number of transmutations had to take place, roughly approximating the cultural transvaluations from earlier heroic incarnations. Steve Austin was an astronaut all right, but that fact only represents a previous existence, lofty and pregnant with heroic possibilities, but largely an unfulfilled pre-identity. After a near-fatal or ordinarily fatal crash, he is given new life by strange, miraculous, and secret methods. As the "bionic man" he has an enormous price tag on his existence. Thus the traditional values of heroic origin have been transmuted by the contemporary alchemy. Steve is heroic in nature because he combines ancient virtues and futuristic technology in the immediate knowledge of how much it cost to make him.

The makers of "The Six Million Dollar Man" have been very careful in projecting inoffensive heroic qualities for a mass audience. Steve Austin is consistently neither a loner, rebel, anti-establishment, bring-about-a-new-order figure like Billy Jack and Kwai Chang (Kung Fu) Caine nor a slickly comforting company man, an old-order law-and-order establishmentarian-authoritarian-in-place-in-the-hierarchy-of-power like Kojak and the Blue Knight. He isn't even a Neitzschean combination of the two like Dirty Harry. Instead, in his understated way, he is almost all things to almost all people. He can be high-mindedly individualistic or nobly selfless; he can be admirably rational or sympathetically emotional/intuitive; he can be loyal either to friend or to institution. As a hero with qualities he is a mighty shape-shifter, but a chameleon in pastels.

Is his popularity due to a recognition of pluralistic value systems in our culture? I think not. All these heroic qualities are peripheral to the one constant in his heroic image, his identity in terms of dollars in seven figures. In effect, however, Steve Austin is a top-rated hero not for what he is but for what he does. The qualities are contingent upon the feats; the narrative scenarios are constructed for the feats, and the qualities are adapted like conventional protective coloring. And here is where the makers of "The Six Million Dollar Man" have shown their genius and where George Steiner would find his astronaut hero if he looked with less elitist eyes.

Steve Austin is heroic for what he does. And what he does is to show week after week that he is the greatest athlete of all. Six million is a bargain for superjock. In every episode, he manages to demonstrate that he can run faster, jump higher, throw farther, and lift or bend or push or break more strongly than any other human. With an unerring grasp of the American pulse they have made an ideal hero for a sports-minded society. They have given us a measure of our ideals, a statistical champion who is whatever we want him to be (and whom we accept for whatever he might be at the time) because of what he does. And to lend credence to the creation both the actors who portray the bionic wunder-couple, Lindsay Wagner and Lee Majors, and the characters themselves, Jaime Sommers and Steve Austin, are authenticated by athletic backgrounds.

In this way TV's fictional hero is a mirror of the process by which athletic figures are made into heroes. The feats take precedence and immediate prominence. The substance of sports reporting is the performance of athletes—the records, the statistics. And the media, the contemporary vehicles of myth, elevate athletic results to heroic feats at the slightest provocation. Coincidentally—that is, coinciding with the price-tag element of Steve Austin's superjock heroism—many sports champions earn their crowns by earning the most dollars. Golf, tennis, bowling, rodeo—they produce and measure their heroes by a monolithic money dimension.

If the statistics and exploits are compiled and exploited to fashion heroic feats, then how is the element of qualities in traditional heroic myth accommodated? The answer to this question is really the demonstration of contemporary myth-making processes at work. It is a matter of imagination, having little if anything to do with the true nature of the people involved.

All that is necessary for the myth to begin is a name and numbers. Imagination accomplishes the rest. Let a jock set a record, compile impressive figures of wins or percentages or prize money, and he is fair game for a legend. Perhaps the media take over and, drawing attention to the feats, imply or consciously create the qualities. Perhaps the PR game begins to be played, an image projected upon the screen of a hero-hungry, hero-consuming public. Or perhaps the creative imagination of the public itself, having inherited the myth-forming process, grants the statistically fashioned heroes *in potentia* whatever qualities they need for their apotheosis.

Many athletes have a quality that makes it easy for creative imaginations to enrich their hero image. It is a palpable but indefinable quality called charisma. Ordinarily some personal contact is necessary for the charismatic quality to be projected, but a few have the ability to project it on film or TV or even on tape or radio or photograph, especially when they get the kind of overexposure that flatters and enriches our outstanding athletes. I can best describe charisma by my own experience, especially since I am not generally susceptible to hero worship or supranatural emanations.

In the presence of three athletes I have experienced a sense of presences that extended beyond the physical dimensions of their bodies. It was clearly not a matter of size, though two of the athletes were large men, Muhammad Ali and Westley Unseld. The third was Bill Shoemaker. These men seemed to me larger than life. Their energy bodies, as George Leonard might put it, filled the space around them and dominated large rooms. I felt what was almost the pressure of a power that radiated from within them. And in each case the feeling was strongest when the men were quiet and their bodies still. In repose, these figures projected a sense of enormous energy and strength and will.

Perhaps this sounds like just so much romantic blather, but I report these experiences as objectively as I can in order to testify concretely to a quality, charisma, that is usually defined only abstractly. Charisma is another one of those ubiquitous Greek words, meaning a special gift or grace divinely bestowed. We have stripped away the divine origin from our semantic associations with charisma, but we have replaced it with the notion of "natural, innate" excellence. Charisma cannot be learned, developed, or conferred. It comes from within a person who is perceived as having the *capacity* to perform great feats. But just as clearly, my perceptions of Ali, Shoemaker, and Unseld in repose were enhanced if not actually formed by my knowledge of and admiration for what they had performed in their sports. From my own perspective I should probably add that their natures as I experienced them were neither contaminated nor compromised when separated from their special, protected world of sports.

These are difficult times for heroes, even sporting ones. Our society seems to want to cut everyone down to size. We seek out imperfections, exult in flaws, and sneer at foibles. We even pretend to like public figures for their weaknesses, which is a kind of inverse narcissism. George Solomon, sports editor of the *Washington Post*, talked about this when he visited my class. His example was Sonny Jurgensen, as popular a local hero as you could find: "Everyone around here loves Sonny in his devil-may-care, easy-going role and with his big gut. So what if Sonny gets caught with a driving charge? That's just a part of Sonny. You, the public, set up these idols."

But don't you, Solomon was asked, raise sports figures to the level of idols by printing items on the sports page about Sonny's politics, Bill Walton's diet, and Tom Payne's rape case? "Maybe we should have a section called Sports Life," he said, adding that these were national sports figures and the paper had an obligation to print it when they do or say something interesting.

Well, then, came the next question, how do you feel about the public's interest in the way sports and sports figures carry over into every other aspect of the society? Does that lead you to question your own devotion to sports or the paper's devotion to sports?

SOLOMON: You devote so many columns a day to sports and you have to have a balance of what you think people are interested in. Now there are those that think you should print nothing else but games. You know, Maryland is going to play North Carolina, write the games, tell us who scored the baskets, ask the coach who won or lost, period. But there are those who are interested in perhaps knowing a little bit about the human beings who play basketball: what they're like, what they have to say, what they think about the particular game, what they think about particular things. Life changes. You've got to feel that what people say and what people are like are as important as what people do—if they're important people.

ISAACS: You're not just reacting to what the public wants, then. Your pages actually steer the public's response, don't they?

SOLOMON: Well, they steer it, but if you steer it on a course that the public doesn't like, you hear about it.

The public reacts strongly against invasions of the sacred world of sports, particularly when the media expose heroic idols to be petty, foolish, flawed, and corrupt. "Say it ain't so, Joe" is a cry of universal anguish. But much of the exposure seems to come when athletic heroes range beyond the confines of sports into more mundane, profane activities. Yet these activities are perceived as the corrupting agents by the hero-worshiping world, rather than having the athletes seem as normally, naturally corrupt individuals who happen to be proficient at some game or event. At times, however, the activities in the profane world may give greater stature to the athlete hero in his sacred world.

Shirley Povich, in his visit to class, spoke about this in relation to Muhammad Ali: "He started off being a hero to the blacks, he's a great fighter and a great champion, but he became the hero, I do believe, most when he defied the draft boards, defied the courts, he defied the whole United States with a simple expression, 'I ain't got nothing against them Vietcongs.' And there he stood as a hero." Povich continued,

> Then, as I said the other day, he proved it in the ring and maybe transcended the fact that nobody likes a braggart who consistently makes good on his boasts, yet he rose above it. He did all that and despite the status of braggart he became popular, and as we know when we learned of him the other day, when we saw him on the program, he does have a superb kind of charm.

Ali had appeared on "Panorama," a local TV talk show, interviewed by Povich and his son Maury. This was followed by a discussion of the athlete as hero with Povich *père et fils,* William Barry Furlong, and me. Reference to the program initiated the following exchange in the classroom interview:

ISAACS: Where do our heroes come from and what are the conditions for the creation of heroes?

POVICH: Well, we have to generalize a bit. We can't quite nail it down but what we do know is that all peoples, and Americans aren't excepted, demand heroes in the same way that they demanded kings, knights, and leaders all through different ages. We have a great willingness to find them and accept them and a little bit of Walter Mitty in all of us so that we can all get the idea that our heroes represent us in some very flattering way. So who are our heroes? I could say they are the ones who beat all the odds.

ISAACS: It seems to me that one necessary element is the ability to fantasize about the individual, that is, the ability to tell stories about him. I guess it's originally a sports cliché, "a legend in his own time." When you make a public figure the subject of a legend, of mythology, you are birthing a hero. Now Ali is the author of his own mythology in a sense; he's his own poet laureate. I think this is one of the most fascinating things about him. It's this Bonnie-and-Clyde element of wanting to tell his own story. He tells it over and over again in a way that makes it a routine, a performance. It's an artistic performance in that it may or may not bear a direct relationship to his biography. It's his number, his bit.

POVICH: Well, I think that's mostly correct. I'd have to say this, that almost without exception—I've never known the case to be otherwise—the legend never came before the hero. The hero must come before the legend and this takes us down to performance. Heroes build their heroism by performance and after that the myths begin to be built up around him and he becomes a legend.

Muhammad Ali with his wonderful repetitive orations has invited the myth and invited the legend and is one in his own time.

ISAACS: It's interesting how the legends develop. I think that as a sportswriter you have to take some credit for the development of legends that follow the performance, the heroic feats that are the substance, the subject of these stories. It's the press that makes the heroes, isn't it?

POVICH: Well I think you're right most of the way. But I'm almost tempted to say that the ones who build the legends are the lousy sportswriters.

ISAACS: Why do you say this?

POVICH: Too often we can get lyrical about too little and lack an objectivity and forget, as we like to say, after all it's just a game, not life or death, and in a couple of years it'll be forgotten and not for posterity or eternity. Another will come along. . . . Too many sportswriters are fans themselves.

ISAACS: One thing that I find very interesting about legendary feats in sports is how many people claim to have witnessed them. You ever notice how many people claim to have been there when Bobby Thomson hit his home run?

POVICH: I can give you a better example.

ISAACS: I hope you're not going to tell me about the number of Philistines who claimed they were there when Samson brought the house down.

POVICH: I can't go back quite that far, but I can go back a few years. When I came to Washington in the twenties, Walter

Johnson was a great hero, and I personally ran into something like twenty-three thousand people who would say, "I
was there when Walter Johnson pitched his first game."
Fine. I took the trouble to look up the box score in 1907 and
there were twelve hundred and four present, and twenty-
three thousand claimed to have seen it.

I think that's fairly typical. People delude themselves.
First they make a lying boast and in time they end up believ-
ing they actually were there.

Later, in response to a student's question, Povich expanded
on the fascinating figure of Ali:

I could tell you a case which would illustrate the affection in which
this man was held, particularly by the blacks, and this was not in
America, this was in Jamaica. In March of 1973, I went down there
to cover the Joe Frazier–George Foreman fight, a fight between
two blacks. Jamaicans had never seen either one of them, and Ali
was nowhere on the scene. As Frazier and Foreman moved in
there, Jamaica, Foreman was the instant favorite, not so much to
win the fight, but he was the man Jamaicans were hoping to win the
fight.

Why? They wanted to see him beat the man who beat Ali. This is
what they based their affection on. Frazier, just as black, even
blacker than Ali, had licked their hero. And anybody who could lick
Frazier was the new hero, and this was why they just acclaimed the
fact that Foreman did knock Frazier out.

But Povich is primarily a baseball man, who likes to rehearse
Red Smith's observation that baseball is a dull game only for
those with dull minds. I asked him, "Is it likely that we'll ever see
public acceptance of baseball heroes to the degree that we once
had—Babe Ruth, Joe DiMaggio, Teddy Ballgame?"

Shall we ever get the same great universal acceptance of baseball
heroes that we had in the age of Ruth and Ty Cobb and Walter
Johnson and Teddy Williams or DiMaggio? I don't think so, for a

very special reason. When they were the big stars, Ruth particularly, we might almost say that baseball was the only game in town. There was a great focus on the one big sport of America and that is our national game. But now sports interest is so fragmented and diffused that you can almost have your choice of sports, and nobody is going to overwhelm the scene in any one sport as happened in the days of Ruth, Cobb, Johnson, and DiMaggio. And I think maybe that's the simplest explanation of why we don't get the ready acceptance of the individual heroes that we had in those former years.

I asked him if the players themselves aren't equally great, and he said that they are maybe better, that the modern baseball players are better in many respects. "There are more good pitchers and many better fielders, but I don't think that there are as many good hitters."

The increasing speed at which conditions change produces a parade of heroes at quick-march. Lipsyte has commented on this in a way that implies some essential perceptions about the sacred world of sports and the public's ardent defense thereof:

> The athlete is a hero at sufferance, controllable and disposable. Dead ones, like Ruth, are even better than old ones who could, presumably, commit racial slurs or be caught fondling children in YMCA bathrooms, or, worst of all, complain. The hero as object gives us role models we can manipulate, notches in time as nostalgic as old hit tunes, and diverting amusement. Sportswriters, presumably speaking for their constituents, the fans, react badly against holdouts, strikes, and lawsuits by players, because it unmakes the magic: Fans do not really want players to humanize themselves too much.

He then makes mention of the name that often arises in any discussion of the American hero, that of Charles Augustus Lindbergh, the Lone Eagle:

> The Babe's partner in glory that marvelous 1927 season, Charles Lindbergh, died in the summer of 1974. After several generations of bad press he was making a comeback as a hero of conservation.

But I don't think he would have made it; the superlatives necessary to distinguish Lindbergh from contemporary celebrities had been devalued in his lifetime, and they no longer packed the power to convince us.

Lipsyte noted that Harry Reasoner in a TV obit called Lindbergh "a legend in his lifetime" but that later the same night, Frank Gifford called Paul Brown "a legend in his own time." And then he wondered at how small a chance Lindy would have had against "all those other living legends, those men larger than life, those TV immortals" from SportsWorld.

At this point I would again make a brief comparison of our culture with Latin America. My guest was Wally Keiderling who through various travels, studies, grants, and appointments with the USIA and the Foreign Service has spent much of his adult life in Guatemala, Bolivia, the Dominican Republic, and Paraguay. During this time he has also kept up an active interest in sports. A collegiate wrestler at Oklahoma A. & M., he has coached basketball and volleyball in Latin America, pitched for the Dominican national softball team, and used sports to promote understanding and cooperation through various diplomatic missions.

I asked him, "Whom do the Dominicans regard as a hero in their culture?"

He said, "In the first place, Trujillo is not. Even to his followers, he would not be as much a hero as Juan Marichal." He went on to talk about the visibility of the Alous, Manny Mota, Marichal, and Rico Carty to Domenicanos, providing them with their one model of escape from the cane fields. As heroes they are icons of freedom from an oppressive, empty existence. He presented similar examples from other Latin American cultures.

In his view, most Latin athletes care greatly about winning as a prime demonstration of machismo. Awards for sportsmanship are uncommon, because the very idea of being a good sport conflicts with macho. Thus the Latin invests a great deal of his sense of honor—national and municipal as well as personal honor—in athletic competition, and this is particularly true of the sports of the people (as opposed to the golf, tennis, and swimming of the upper classes), such as soccer, baseball, boxing, wrestling, volleyball, and basketball in proportions appropriate to the particular locale.

The outstanding athlete is consequently a natural culture hero, whose sporting prowess is automatically accompanied by the embodiment of honored qualities. Financial rewards are not influential and with rare exceptions (Pele, for example) are relatively slight, so that the role of hero is *in itself* a motivation for athletic aspirations. The point of contrast for us is this: the sacred world of sports in Latin America is universally acknowledged as separate and sacrosanct; its heroes are measured and honored qualitatively; and it makes no cultural or social sense to extrapolate from one world to the other, from sacred to profane or vice versa, to confuse athletics with commerce or politics or the arts. But in our culture we continually confuse issues and transpose values, often substituting quantity for quality, and sometimes actively seeking to break down what might be considered natural boundaries.

This process of confusion or the destruction of mythic values often provokes strong reaction from an outraged public. For example, late in 1975 the *Washington Star* ran a series on "Homosexuals in Sports" by Lynn Rosellini. If the stories themselves had been less innocuous they might have been called irresponsible, but the general conclusion was that athletes, like any other group that could be isolated in our society, reflected the society as a whole in its percentage of homosexuals. But like certain other rather specialized occupational groups, professional women golfers and tennis players tended to include a percentage of homosexuals far above the norm. Very few names were mentioned, no lurid details were presented, and it was clear that the homosexual athletes were more concerned about their public image than about any such avant-garde notion as gay liberation.

They were right to be concerned. The response to the series

was overwhelmingly negative. People wrote and called to protest the damage done to the athletes' images in children's minds. "Have a little regard for the young, impressionable boys and girls who are so awestruck with these heroes," wrote a woman from Falls Church. And a man who rejoiced in the way kids' identification with "their heroes transcends race" went on about where models are not to be found:

> Kids today will hesitate to admit wanting to be soldiers (murderers), federal agents or policemen (burglars), blue-collar workers (unemployed), small businessmen (broke), doctors (sued), or President (crook). Thanks for messing with the image of the pro athlete.

A caller said, simply, "There are gay people everywhere. Why in the sports pages? It's a sacred page."

Commenting on the response to the series, Jane O'Reilly said in her December 14 column, "Sports is the place for myth, sacred cows, untouchables, ancestor worship and ritualization of trivia." Her point of view as militant feminist focuses on the sports pages' glorification of the sports industry, which depends "on a basic marketing concept of pure macho: aggressiveness, winning, hard living" and projects the image of "Mythic Masculine Hero." But take the sexism out of the argument and it still retains its force. The sports pages chronicle a sacred world and only therein are larger-than-life figures maintained as a matter of course, universally acceptable.

Any attempt to cut these figures down to human size is offensive and intolerable. While political and entertainment figures are fair game for debunkers, and the public rejoices in the public airing of their dirty laundry and clay feet, the only acceptable "human interest" material about jocks concerns quirks or foibles or oddities that enhance their legendary nature. The marriages of Joe DiMaggio and Marilyn Monroe, Lance Rentzel and Joey Heatherton, Bo Belinsky and Mamie van Doren, and Terry Bradshaw and JoJo Starbuck were made in the sacred heavens of sports mythmaking. But let there be nothing kinky about them. In Heatherton, Rentzel had a fine trophy, a "perfect sleeper" of an image for a jock myth. But when his psychosexual problems are exposed, we don't want to hear about it on the sports pages and we don't want him playing in our big league any more.

Sports mythology is deliberately archaic, its heroes throwbacks to golden ages of purity and incorruptibility. The old virtues and the eternal verities are embodied in them. They symbolize qualities we'd still like to admire but can't hardly find any more. A scurrilous demythologizing may suggest a heavy use of drugs by athletes, especially professional football players. But before such a destructive idea can take root in an anguished public fancy, the NFL launches an antidrug campaign in the public interest, with scores of its star players taping little antidrug sermonettes. And even the most cynical sports fan swallows it.

Professional sport can boast of how issues of race are transcended in its blue serene, and to maintain that exemplary image of color blindness it must squash all rumors of racial dissension on teams. (Remember that vigorous denials on sports pages are consistently as close to admissions or confessions as one can get on those pages, as many fired coaches and managers can testify. A vote of confidence means that one can confidently expect a pink slip.) But where the possibility exists for a genuinely meaningful gesture toward interracial understanding, it will frighten the sports world into a conspiracy of silence.

Consider the case of a superstar outfielder who might be inexplicably traded away at the height of his career and ability. The player could end up an exile, having lost his court fight against the reserve clause, but the reason for the trade might never come to light. It would never be fit for public ears to hear that a beautiful black player indulged in sexual liaisons with beautiful white women. And it would never be fit for the public image of a professional baseball team that racial integration could be carried that far.

Baseball could never tolerate even the less-than-new morality according to which married players might discover teammates' wives to be more congenial than their own. They might make honest men and women of themselves by divorces and remarriage, but they won't be retained on the same roster.

The sports establishment will go to absurd extremes to retain the image of purity from an old-world, last-century concept of public morality. And these efforts may be counterproductive in terms of retaining images of heroism. Witness the "public apologies" of Cleon Jones and Joe Namath. Jones, the most consistently excellent outfielder in Met history, apologized for conduct unbecoming a Met, after legal charges against him had been dismissed. According to reports, he had been arrested for indecent exposure after police had caught him in a van with a young woman. The woman was black, so that was no problem, and her youth only made her a suitable object of macho-heroic attention. Nor need the fact that Jones was married have mattered, since gods and heroes are famously prodigal with their virility. The problems were (1) that he was *caught,* like any common public nuisance; (2) that he was caught in a *van,* with its overtones of counterculture and hippydom; and (3) that he was over the hill in a baseball—not marital—sense, so that if his hero image could be cut so could his hero-level salary.

With Namath, on the other hand, the sports establishment had actually traded on his image as rebel hero. He was the new breed, the long-haired, free-spirited swinger who could be a viable folk hero for new generations of NFL addicts. Never mind the obviously bourgeois values of Namath's actual life style and mind set; never mind that Namath could be wholeheartedly embraced as the rightful inheritor of the blue-collar, Archie Bunker generation; the point was that he could be sold, merchandized, and mythologized as antiestabishment proof that pro football was with it.

But the antiestablishment posture can only go so far. Namath went too far. In the sacred world, the triumph over the old order is the laudatory feat, the stuff of saga. Joe Willie would boast that he would beat Unitas and the Colts, the champion representatives of the old order, and he would carry out his boast. The quick release of mouth and pass made him a mythic hero. But in the profane world, where his interest in a cabaret, Bachelors III, brought him into contact with characters deemed undesirable (and unheroworthy) by the NFL, a quick release of his holdings was demanded. And achieved. With public apology. The myth of the antiestablishment hero was one thing, but in a real confrontation the establishment put the hero in his place and the publican out of his place. If he wanted to continue as a hero it would have to be on conventionally acceptable terms.

The conventions of sports heroism may be enormously broad—liberal in the extreme—as long as they are kept within the bounds of the sacred world. Within those bounds, virtually every mythic scenario may be entertained. The ex-con who makes good in the big leagues is a male Cinderella figure. His crimes against society may have been inadequately paid for, but they are transcended by his ability to steal bases and run down fly balls.

Somewhat more difficult to tolerate are the former heroes whose fall from the sacred world is into the depths of the profane. Beau Jack, a beautiful fighting machine as the lightweight champion, is discovered shining shoes in a pathetic middle age. He becomes thereby the stuff of legendary pathos. His fall from the boxing grace of his prime, the magic circle of the square ring, is a classic loss of high place in the sportsminded mythos. And Hurricane Jackson is pictured in Alan Dugan's poem as shattered in face and mind, with one ear "clenched like a fist" listening to itself, while "someone else, his perfect youth,/laureled in newsprint and dollar bills,/triumphs forever on the great white way/to the statistical Sparta of the champs."

Jackson's characterization is easy, like Beau Jack's, but that of another Hurricane, Carter, blows up a much more complex storm. If the ascension of a Ron Laflore or a Willy Horton or a

Jim Rivera or a Sonny Liston or even a Don King from prison to athletic triumph is a tribute to the sanctifying power of the sacred world of sports, what can be made of the descent of a man from a highly ranked contender to a felony-murder convict? Taking Dylan's song and the well-organized campaign to free Hurricane Carter as manifestations of myth, i.e., setting aside the question (which I can't presume to answer) of whether or not he was guilty of any crime against society, in a legal sense, in the real world, I would argue that he has become a type of the sacrificial victim, the scapegoat. First, his fall is tragic in the simple way that Beau Jack's was, a fall from high place in the sacred world and then out of that world into the profane. Then the fall is complicated when he is punished for it by becoming a victim of profane institutions—society, law and order, racial prejudice. And when the victimization is celebrated in the mythic scenarios of the media, he is apotheosized once again as a tragic sports hero.

Only if his crime were against the sacred world itself would his heroic nature be transformed into baser stuff by the de-mythologizing process. Jack Molinas, whose legend could have been that of a supreme rogue-hero because of his performances on and off the basketball court and his ultimate assassination in modern-gangland style, lost his stature by being named the master fixer in one of the major basketball scandals. Ralph Beard and Alex Groza, Sherman White and Ed Warner, among many others, have been read out of the roster of heroes for alleged point-shaving. But even in this company, exceptions may be made to fit a mythic scenario. Thus Floyd Layne, who slipped from glory to infamy for his part in the 1950 basketball fixes, has become a hero of the redemptive power of the sacred world. He never left it; working at great personal sacrifice in the remotest basketball vineyards out of his love for the game, he has won the storybook reward of the head coaching job at the institution he once exalted and betrayed.

The stories of athletic heroes do not often end in triumph. They may die young in their prime or broken in age, but heroes they remain in the stories left behind, resurrected or recreated in the clear vision of hindsight. The All-American boy might end up the dirty old man, but as long as he doesn't befoul the sacred terrain—or as long as the mythologizers of that realm keep the lid on his peccadilloes or make light of his flaws—his legend maintains the luster of his eminence.

More shimmering than most because more ephemeral and insubstantial are the legendary images of the heroes that could have been, the stars manqués, tragically aborted in their atheltic careers by the hard realities of the profane world. And so are celebrated in song and story the wondrous exploits of a Bernard Levi, whose moves were so marvelous that Dave Bing couldn't carry his jock when they were back in Spingarn High School, or an Earl Manigault, whose playground performances promised that he would have put the Hawk and Dr. J in the shade if he ever won his place in the sun. But only their legendary promise lives in the sacred world, because the street, the system, and the drugs never let them pass beyond the profane.

It sometimes requires the services of a major artist to perpetuate a myth that flacks find too much for their typically simplistic notions. Here is Randall Jarrell's poem, "Say Good-bye to Big Daddy," not an elegy by any means, in the traditional sense, but a matter-of-mythic-fact statement about his nature and passing:

> Big Daddy Lipscomb, who used to help them up
> After he'd pulled them down, so that "the children
> Won't think Big Daddy's mean"; Big Daddy Lipscomb,
> Who stood unmoved among the blockers, like the Rock
> Of Gibralter in a life insurance ad,
> Until the ball carrier came, and Daddy got him;
> Big Daddy Lipscomb, being carried down an aisle
> Of women by Night Train Lane, John Henry Johnson,
> And Lenny Moore; Big Daddy, his three ex-wives,
> His fiancée, and the grandfather who raised him
> Going to his grave in five big Cadillacs;
> Big Daddy, who found football easy enough, life hard enough

To—after his last night cruising Baltimore
In his yellow Cadillac—to die of heroin;
Big Daddy, who was scared, he said: "I've been scared
Most of my life. You wouldn't think so to look at me.
It gets so bad I cry myself to sleep—" his size
Embarrassed him, so that he was helped by smaller men
And hurt by smaller men; Big Daddy Lipscomb
Has helped to his feet the last ball carrier, Death.

The big black man in the television set
Whom the viewers stared at—sometimes, almost were—
Is a blur now; when we get up to adjust the set,
It's not the set, but a NETWORK DIFFICULTY.
The world won't be the same without Big Daddy.
Or else it will be.

Big Daddy Lipscomb was something of an anomaly for pro football's PR long before he ODed. There was an uneasiness about his gentleness and sensitivity. There has always been room in the sacred world for images of the gentle giant, but somehow it didn't go down easy with the flamboyant life style and the colorful execution of his duties as defensive lineman.

That uneasiness about confusion of role and personality remains. It is evidenced by a kind of embarrassed joking about athletic figures who take on an extra dimension that doesn't fit the forms or formulas. The NFL uneasily dealt with the image of Mike Reid, the Cincinnati Bengal linebacker whose ambition was to be a concert pianist. The idea was to broaden the image of the football player in a pluralistic culture, but the discomfort of the football establishment probably came from the subclinical itch that the sacred world was being infected by the multidimensional practicality of the profane. An ad for the yellow pages featuring Lou Brock and his flower shop or the image of DiMag puttering around the house making coffee brought a similar itch, almost as nagging as Namath in pantyhose.

The extreme position against deviation into pluralism is demonstrated in the following exchange of letters. The first was addressed to Minnesota Twins manager Frank Quilici from John Preston, editor of the *San Mateo Advocate*, the "largest gay publication in the United States":

> we are expanding our editorial content to include sports news and personalities. As the major vehicle for gay people's self-image, we are very concerned with presenting positive role models to our readership. . . . Could you help us by letting us know which of your ball players are living a gay lifestyle? I would appreciate it if your publicity department would set up interviews with them for us.

Tom Mee answered for the Twins:

> I can't think of a more disgusting or revolting possibility for professional sports than that suggested in your letter. The cop-out, immoral life style of the tragic misfits espoused by your publication has no place in organized athletics at any level. Your colossal gall in attempting to extend your perversion to an area of total manhood is just simply unthinkable.

The "area of total manhood" is blighted by frequent tremors and terrors and often overreacts in violent aftershocks.

The macho image and the accompanying product identification so dear to the hearts of athletes' agents and market researchers were endangered by all these kinds of extradimensioning. The countercampaign reinforced the old values. A light beer commercial has John Mackey and Matt Snell arm wrestling in a positive display, and another has Mickey Mantle and Whitey Ford trading on the blasphemous Bouton notions by joking about their heroic limitations as drinkers. More significant was the ad that laughed to scorn the idea of Dick Butkus's sensitivity.

Best of all was the tableau of Ben Davidson, Roosevelt Grier, and Ray Nitschke sitting in rocking chairs and doing needlepoint. Grier is notorious for his countermacho image. In fact, one of the most devastating of defensive tackles in his playing prime, he has become an articulate, authentic spokesman for needlepoint. But now, flanked by two all-pro superbrutes, Grier was put in the position of ridiculing his own identity.

No wonder Big Daddy Lipscomb was a problem for the image makers and the image protectors. The unmoved tackler "who used to help them up" was not simply a gentle giant, because off field his neon-technicolor style didn't accord with that image. Jarrell makes a clear consistency of the apparent incongruities. Lipscomb played at life in the profane world as he played football in the sacred—like a child. A pure innocent, who could neither compartmentalize worlds and roles nor deal in sophisticated gradations of values and accommodations, Big Daddy could not compromise; Big Daddy could not mix motivations with the simple game he played in; and Big Daddy could not handle the fear that loomed as big as his person over the puny insignifiance of his reality.

Jarrell understood the larger importance, too. He recognized the mass identification with the massive performer on the Sunday screen. The world that Jarrell says "won't be the same without Big Daddy" is the real world in which an individual who may have touched people in a real place will be missed. But when he says, finally, "Or else it will be," he focuses our attention on the other world which will always be the same, outside of time, apart from the reality of the individual.

In that world, Big Daddy Lipscomb retains his identity as a gentle giant. With Big Daddy himself no longer actively playing the role of that mythic hero, it is played by others. And always will be. And that is why a poem written to "Say Good-bye to Big Daddy" can never be a proper elegy.

# III

# THE LAUREL
# AND THE IVY

The last chapter discussed the myth-making function of the mass media, the way they take sports figures and make them the subjects of heroic scenarios and the embodiments of heroic virtues. It is equally important for an understanding of the phenomena of hero making in our jockocracy to examine the role of creative artists and the image of the hero in imaginative narrative. Here it is easier, and perhaps somewhat more comfortable for a critic, to chart a process of change and transvaluation.

"You gotta be a football hero," says the 1933 song by Al Sherman, Al Lewis, and Buddy Fields (published by Leo Feist, popularized by the ol' professor, Ben Bernie), "to get along with the beautiful girls. You gotta be a touchdown getter, you bet, if you wanna get a baby to pet." The naïveté of this attitude, oversimplified in a juvenile lyric, is nevertheless reflected in generations of serious literature. The narrator of E. L. Doctorow's *Ragtime* says,

> Of course at this time in our history [ca. 1910] the images of ancient
> Egypt were stamped on everyone's mind. This was due to the discov-

eries being reported out of the desert by British and American archaeologists. After the football players in their padded canvas knee pants and leather helmets, archaeologists were the glamour personages of the Universities.

The historical accuracy of Doctorow's presentation has been called in question on rather dubious aesthetic grounds, but there is no doubt of his capacity to focus on prevailing social and cultural attitudes through sharply drawn details. The phrase I would draw attention to here is "stamped on everyone's mind." We are not talking about real heroes and concrete accomplishments; we are talking about public perceptions and the way they are produced—sometimes by the creation and perpetuation of fantasies.

The football hero was a fantasy that seemed peculiarly congenial to America, and we seem even now to be reluctant to let it go, preferring modifications and adjustments to anything resembling rejection. Walker Percy in *The Moviegoer* suggests part of its appeal, a nostalgia for a lost golden time:

> [Uncle Jules] and Walter talk football. Uncle Jules' life ambition is to revive the fortunes of the Tulane football team. I enjoy the talk because I like football myself and especially do I like to hear Uncle Jules tell about the great days of Jerry Dalrymple and Don Zimmerman and Billy Banker. When he describes a goal-line stand against L.S.U. in 1932, it is like King Arthur standing fast in the bloodred sunset against Sir Modred and the traitors. Walter was manager of the team and so he and Uncle Jules are thick as thieves.

The very names of past players are able to summon up romantic, heroic images in the minds of sports-aware people. To anyone who was alive to sports before World War I, for example, the name of Hobey Baker evokes—more than time and place—a feeling of grandeur and a sense of heroism much larger than the life of a Princeton football and hockey player.

As George Frazier has said, in the Prologue to John D. Davies's book, *The Legend of Hobey Baker* (1966),

You say "Hobey Baker" and all of a sudden you see the gallantry of a world long since gone—a world of all the sad young men, a world in which handsome young officers spent their leaves tea-dancing at the Plaza to the strains of the season; a world in which poets sang of their rendezvous with death when spring came round with rustling shade and apple blossoms filled the air.

It was a world in which young men soared into the sky and fell in flames. There was such gallantry, such great grace in that world. That was Hobey Baker's world, and it is good that it is not forgotten. For if it seems odd how his name keeps coming up after all these years, it is an oddness devoutly to be desired. And on days like this one, it bespeaks our return, if only for a little while, to the time before we all of us fell from grace.

Davies has confronted those feelings and faced them unashamed. It is a biography of a legend, not a life, so that analysis is virtually set aside. But Davies gives two reasons to account for the perpetuation of the legend:

his life has a fabulous, inevitable, dramatic quality about it, like a Greek tragedy. His death seems like that of a Greek tragic hero, typically destroyed by his own tragic flaw—reckless courage—which is at the same time the source of his strength. . . .

The other explanation is historical: in our modern age which refuses to believe in heroes, his name has ironically taken on a special antique patina, as connoting not just the best in American sport and sportsmanship, but in addition the "old-fashioned" qualities of decency, modesty, kindness, courtesy—the qualities of the gentleman—the avatar of an earlier, better day, an age of innocence, an age of faith.

The case is supported by a passage from Al Lang, writing in the *New York Herald Tribune* in 1952:

Hobey Baker was for the American youth a hero in the truest sense, godlike almost in his stature. It was as though the gods had fashioned one shining symbol in their own image towards which boys should strive in the future. He was a sort of legendary hero like Sir Galahad, Richard the Lion-Hearted and even Paul Bunyan, for his athletic feats were legendary too.

And it is extended in the Introduction by Arthur Mizener, who called Hobey the "Sir Philip Sidney or . . . the Major Robert Gregory of his age" and concluded with this suggestion:

> With his almost incredible skill and grace, his perfect manners, his dedicated seriousness, Hobey Baker was the nearly faultless realization of the ideal of his age. To understand him is to understand an age to which we owe more than we like to admit. If that age's idea of greatness seems to us in some ways inadequate, we ought to remind ourselves how much it has nonetheless contributed to our idea of greatness, insofar as that idea is represented by men like Adlai Stevenson, Dean Acheson, and John Kennedy, who were significantly influenced by the Princeton, the Yale, and the Harvard for which Hobey Baker was the perfect hero.

What is not sufficiently stressed by Davies, but implied in the book about Hobey's legend and in those called to witness on its behalf, is how much it owes to F. Scott Fitzgerald. Hobey may embody all that we fantacize about the era and all that we imagine of its values, but those perceptions have been codified, recorded, and passed down for us by Fitzgerald. This is not a coincidental association. Fitzgerald idolized Baker, wrote about him specifically, modeled a character on him, and borrowed his second name, Amory, for his protagonist in *This Side of Paradise.*

Fitzgerald's two-word sentence—"Football weather"—sums up the character Charlie Wales's whole perception of environment in "Babylon Revisited" and suggests the depths of the writer's feelings for the sport itself. Indeed, in his 1927 essay "Princeton," Fitzgerald said that the Princeton he knew and belonged to was somehow "bound up" with "the rise of American football":

For at Princeton, as at Yale, football became, back in the 'nineties, a sort of symbol. Symbol of what? Of the eternal violence of American life? Of the eternal immaturity of the race? The failure of a culture within the walls? Who knows? It became something at first satisfactory, then essential and beautiful. It became, long before the insatiable millions took it, with Gertrude Ederle and Mrs. Snyder, to its heart, the most intense and dramatic spectacle since the Olympic games. The death of Johnny Poe with the Black Watch in Flanders starts the cymbals crashing for me, plucks the strings of nervous violins as no adventure of the mind that Princeton ever offered. A year ago in the Champs Elysées I passed a slender dark-haired young man with an indolent characteristic walk. Something stopped inside me; I turned and looked after him. It was the romantic Buzz Law whom I had last seen one cold fall twilight in 1915, kicking from behind his goal line with a bloody bandage round his head.

Football images pervade *This Side of Paradise.* Near the end Amory, in a funk, thinks, "Life was a damned muddle . . . a football game with every one off-side and the referee gotten rid of— every one claiming the referee would have been on his side. . . ." Life properly, apparently, should be a football game played properly, as Hobey Baker would have played it and lived it. And for Amory the model is Allenby, the football captain, whom Fitzgerald modeled explicitly on Baker, seen through worshipful eyes in an epiphanous image:

There at the head of the white platoon marched Allenby, the football captain, slim and defiant, as if aware that this year the hopes of the college rested on him, that his hundred-and-sixty pounds were expected to dodge to victory through the heavy blue and crimson lines.

It is clear that Fitzgerald did not invent the cultic attitude toward football. In fact, he lived it first and only wrote about it in terms of his own perceived reality later. Mizener's biography,

*The Far Side of Paradise* (1951), makes this plain as it describes
the formative backgrounds of Fitzgerald's ideas and attitudes:

> This vision of the heroic athlete was rapidly given an elaborate
> context by the boys' books he read and acquired a heavy burden of
> conventonal detail. The hero was a prep-school or college boy, a
> male cinderella, small and discriminated against, who by some dra-
> matic and unlikely display of pluck won the big game for St. Regis
> or Princeton. This dream was only gradually modified and never
> wholly uprooted by the hard realities of prep-school and college
> life. It put him on the Newman football team despite his dislike of
> the game and sent him out for Freshman football at Princeton—at
> one hundred and thirty-eight pounds. Every so often the ideal
> would achieve a new personification: Sam White in the Princeton-
> Harvard game of 1911; Hobey Baker, the Princeton captain of 1913
> "slim and defiant"; "the romantic Buzz Law. . . ." In these figures
> he found, as he put it once about Hobey Baker, "an ideal worthy of
> everything in my enthusiastic admiration, yet consummated and
> expressed in a human being who stood within ten feet of me."

Mizener tells the familiar story of how Fitzgerald chose Princeton because of a score of a Triangle Club show. But he adds a
footnote about another score, because Fitzgerald himself sometimes said that it was seeing Sam White beat Harvard that decided him for Princeton. "White's touchdown," Mizener grants,
"was exactly the kind of sudden, brilliant, individual act which
would have struck his imagination, especially as it occurred for
him against a background of gallant defeats." And this explanation also accords with Fitzgerald's notion of "the Princeton men
as slender and keen and romantic, and the Yale men as brawny
and brutal and powerful."

It would be a mistake to suppose that the cultic attitude
toward football was peculiar to Fitzgerald among American writers
though it may be accurate to say that it is more apparent in the
texture of his work than in other major authors. It is more important to understand that football had been mythologized to such

an extent in American culture that the romanticized attitudes toward it were taken for granted. It is virtually a given of the set of attitudes projected through Willy Loman in Arthur Miller's *Death of a Salesman.* Thus, Philip Roth's gentle satire of it in *Goodbye, Columbus* succeeded because the myth was still very much alive and everywhere acknowledged.

But Fitzgerald recognized the dark side of the myth, its dangerous implications of brutality, and its elevation of sophomoric values. In *The Great Gatsby,* Nick Carraway's first reference to Tom Buchanan says that he, "Among various physical accomplishments, had been one of the most powerful ends that ever played football at New Haven—a national figure in a way, one of those men who reach such an acute limited excellence at twenty-one that everything afterward savors of anti-climax."

This theme of "acute limited excellence" in athletics and the anticlimax of later life has been a popular one. A. E. Housman's "To an Athlete Dying Young," perhaps the best-known poem of *A Shropshire Lad,* presents it ironically in a sense of thankfulness for an untimely early death. The reverse side of the coin—what happens to the athlete-hero who does not die young?—is a subject treated in depth by John Updike in *Rabbit, Run* and *Rabbit Redux,* by Tennessee Williams in *Cat on a Hot Tin Roof,* and by Irwin Shaw in "The Eighty-Yard Run" among many others. Carraway says of Tom that he "would drift on forever seeking, a little wistfully, for the dramatic turbulence of some irrecoverable football game."

Wistfulness, however, is not quite the word for the destruction of living values and of individual lives that accompanies the pathetic failure of a football-fantasy world to accord with the realities of mature experience. Shaw's Christian Darling ends the short story about him in full acceptance of that failure but unable to avoid trying to recapture the fantasy. Williams's Brick Pollitt ends the play about him at a point where maturity is at least possible because the fantasy has finally been shattered.

It is problematic whether *Cat on a Hot Tin Roof* is about

Brick. In Act II it is primarily about Big Daddy and the issue of how to come to terms with his mortality. Enveloping this issue is the problem of Maggie the Cat, and her problem is how to get Brick back into her bed. But both Maggie and Big Daddy must deal with the football myth as personified in Brick and what Williams calls the "conventional mores he got from the world that crowned him with early laurel." Brick's problem is his guilt derived from an earlier conflict between a world in which abhorrence for homosexuality is part of the code and his personal feelings of "real, real, deep, deep friendship" with Skipper.

The Williams play deals peripherally with those elements of violence toward others, toward self, and toward nature that form a constant, implicit counterpoint in the mythologizing of football. In making Buchanan a football player, Fitzgerald raised the tension to the surface. Carraway, again, about Tom:

> Not even the effeminate swank of his riding clothes could hide the enormous power of that body—he seemed to fill those glistening boots until he strained the top lacing, and you could see a great pack of muscle shifting when his shoulder moved under his thin coat. It was a body capable of enormous leverage—a cruel body.

The attractiveness is clear, but it is the cruelty that carries Nick to the point where he can reject the football hero and approve a much different set of values to which Gatsby has vainly clung.

A stage of demythologizing the football fantasy was inevitable. The debunking was presaged, perhaps, by the character of Tom Stark in Robert Penn Warren's *All the King's Men*. A football hero idolized by the masses, he is personally abhorrent to most who know him. Warren has made Tom's football morality and its enactment a cameo of Willie Stark's political ethic and its corrupt application, just as Willie has created Tom in his own image as a useful icon of his power and success. But whereas Warren was allegorizing political, social, and personal morality in the rituals of football, other writers took on the football myth directly and let their satire carry over to the society at large if it would.

In such various satiric portraits of the gridiron as James Thurber's *University Days*, Dan Jenkins's *Semi-Tough*, Pete Gent's *North Dallas Forty*, and Jack Olsen's *Alphabet Jackson*, we find a vigorous demythologizing at work. The basis of these fictions and their appeal to a mass audience as well presuppose a widespread acknowledgment of the myth's existence and acceptance in the first place. If imitation is a form of flattery, mockery surely implies recognition of importance. Even more vigorous than the fictions are the journalistic, biographical, and confessional nonfictions like those by Gary Shaw, Johnny Sample, and Dave Meggyesy (still needed as antidote for the kind of simple-minded adulation found in Jerry Kramer's *Instant Replay*). But so vital a force in our national spirit is football that the demythologizing has given way to a remythologizing.

Three major texts in this movement are *A Fan's Notes* by Frederick Exley, *Joiner* by James Whitehead, and *End Zone* by Don DeLillo. Exley calls his novel a fictional memoir, and the autobiographical narration (whether or not the Frederick Exley who narrates is the same Frederick Exley who collects the royalties, whether the narrated experiences happened to that Frederick or to some other or not at all) reports his intimate identification, in spirit, with Frank Gifford. It is a story of Exley's personal disaster—of his frustrated hunger for fame, of struggles with alcoholism and insanity, of the failure of love. But most of all it is the story of a man whose life is realized not in instants of ecstasy or intellectual illumination (though the memoir is strewn with those), but in moments of contact with Stout Steve Owen, Charlie Conerly, and especially Gifford who, "more than any single person, sustained for me the illusion that fame was possible."

As a budding writer and self-ordained intellectual, Exley chanced to be a USC classmate of Gifford, lusted after Gifford's beautiful girlfriend on occasion, and was once blessed with Gifford's direct, ingenuous smile. As the player goes on to glory with the football Giants the writer passes through crisis after cirsis without ever coming out on the long end of a score. Even at lowest or tensest points, "Gifford and the Giants were all that sustained me, and I lived only from Sunday afternoon to Sunday afternoon." In the stands (on tickets cadged from Conerly) on the day when Bednarik's tackle puts Gifford out for more than a season, he has the truth begin to hit home. Exley eventually learns the bitter lesson of his identity, that "it was my destiny—unlike that of my father, whose fate it was to hear the roar of the crowd—to sit in the stands with most men and acclaim others. It was my fate, my destiny, my end, to be a fan." This is a corrollary of the discovery that, in a sense, Gifford *is* his fame.

For the present argument, what is most significant in the book is Exley's intellectualized account of the sport's appeal:

> Why did football bring me so to life? . . . an island of directness in a world of circumspection. . . . It smacked of something old, something traditional, something unclouded by legerdemain and subterfuge. It had that kind of power over me, drawing me back with the force of something known, scarcely remembered, elusive as integrity—perhaps it was no more than the force of a forgotten childhood. Whatever it was, I gave myself up to the Giants utterly. The recompense I gained was the feeling of being alive.

A counterpoint to the destructive complexities of experience, football provides the quintessential fan with a nourishing set of rituals in which he participates, however vicariously.

In the other two books, the participation in football is active and direct. The intellectual is the football player himself. James Whitehead's exuberant *Joiner* is a novel with the larger-than-life presence of heroic myth. It is a tale in which History, Literature, the South, Race, Justice, Love, Violence, Education, Family, Friendship, and Sex move in a patterned multiple offense against a sophisticated zone defense of Events, Episodes, Ideas, Images, Motifs, Sounds, Smells, Scenes, Sequences, Associations, and

Symbols like so many characters/players in a playlike, gamelike spectacle. The narrator is a 300-pound offensive tackle who elevates each X and O of the whole design to the mythic level.

Joiner himself embodies the complete individual, breaking down the one-dimensional stereotype of the primordial football myth, and constructing in its place a heroic version of the contemporary thinking-feeling man. Even more significant is the way he perceives other football players as representatives of every sophistication, every nuance, of a pluralistic culture. The best example is Joiner's idol, the late Bill Wallick of the Rams:

> a strange man who worked logarithms in his spare time for fun, and a terrible drinker . . . a visionary tackle . . . fascinated by the Möbius strip, a goddamned amateur topologist. . . .
>
> I'd of called him the Platonic Tackle or the Saint of the Interior Line, for he never married, and no man ever easily met his gaze in a game, those pale blue eyes that always seemed to bend around the man he faced. He was always studying the calculus of a perfect block, studying while in the process of playing, his body a harmony of infinite instants, and even his elementary physics was perfect.
>
> . . .
>
> Magnificent!
>
> The greatest topological and drunk master of elementary physics the game will ever see. The plane geometry of yard-markers and first downs, the parabolas of passes, all the mystery of the game's motion was to him a vision, an absurd possibility for human energy and grace—barbaric struggle in Wallick's game was raised to a vivid if not eternal abstraction.

As tightly structured as *Joiner* is ebulliently diffuse but no less poetic in texture, *End Zone* has at its center, Part Two of a tripartite structure, a remarkable telling of a football game between Logos College and West Centrex Biotechnical. It is no surprise that the Word loses to the computerized scientific/technological complex, although the story concerns Logos and its coaches and players, students and faculty. What is surprising is the total capture of the game from the inside (better than ground-level cameras), both the detailed action of the particular game and the sense of playing it—the pain, the brutality, the beauty. We get a play-by-play summary, we get the onomastic delight of play-calling ("Middle-sift-W, alph-set, lemmy-2" and "Blue turk right, double-slot, zero snag delay"), and we get the sounds of the restless natives ("Let's ching those nancies" and "magnolia candy-ass cunt" and "Nigger kike faggot"). And we get the mystical vision of a place-kicker, who says of the game, "It's all double. . . . Double consciousness. Old form superimposed on new. It's a breaking-down of reality. Primitive mirror awareness. Divine electricity. The football feels. The football knows. This is not just one thing we're watching. This is many things."

After the season, when Gary Harkness, the narrator/protagonist, is trying to talk his fellow running-back out of quitting, he talks about what there is of value in football: "The sense of living an inner life right up against the external or tangible life. Of living close to your own skin. You know what I mean. Everything. The pattern. The morality." And earlier, watching a pro game on TV with its slow-motion replays, he perceives that "the game's violence became almost tender, a series of lovely and sensual assaults. The camera held on fallen men, on men about to be hit, on those who did the hitting. It was a lovely relationship with just a trace of mockery; the camera lingered a bit too long, making poetic sport of the wounded."

DeLillo knows just what he is doing, rationalizing the attractiveness of the game, in a process of elevation, into a contemporary, remythologized essence. Yet he is careful also to provide a context in which he lets the reader in on his game. A parenthetical passage prefaces the whole play-by-play:

> The spectator, at this point, is certain to wonder whether he must now endure a football game in print—the author's way of adding his own neat quarter-notch to the scarred bluesteel of combat writing. The game, after all, is known for its assault-technology motif, and numerous commentators have been willing to risk death by analogy

in their public discussions of the resemblance between football and war. But this sort of thing is of little interest to the exemplary spectator. . . . The exemplary spectator is the person who understands that sport is a benign illusion, the illusion that order is possible. It's a form of society that is rat-free and without harm to the unborn; that is organized so that everyone follows precisely the same rules; that is electronically controlled, thus reducing human error and benefiting industry; that roots out the inefficient and penalizes the guilty; that tends always to move toward perfection. The exemplary spectator has his occasional lusts, but not for warfare, hardly at all for that. No, it's details he needs—impressions, colors, statistics, patterns, mysteries, numbers, idioms, symbols. Football, more than other sports, fulfills this need. It is the one sport guided by language, by the word signal, the snap number, the color code, the play name. The spectator's pleasure, when not derived from the action itself, evolves from a notion of the game's unique organic nature. Here is not just order but civilization. And part of the spectator's need is to sort the many levels of material: to allot, to compress, to catalogue. This need leaps from season to season, devouring much of what is passionate and serene in the spectator. He tries not to panic at the final game's final gun. He knows he must retain something, squirrel some food for summer's winter. He feels the tender need to survive the termination of the replay. So maybe what follows is a form of sustenance, a game on paper to be scanned when there are stale days between events; to be propped up and looked at—the book as television set—for whatever is in here of terminology, pattern, numbering. But maybe not. It's possible there are deeper reasons to attempt a play-by-play. The best course is for the spectator to continue forward, reading himself into the very middle of that benign illusion. The author, always somewhat corrupt in his inventions and vanities, has tried to reduce the contest to basic units of language and action. Every beginning, it is assumed, must have a neon twinkle of danger about it, and so grandmothers, sissies, lepidopterists and others are warned that the nomenclature that follows is often indecipherable. This is not the pity it may seem. Much of the appeal of sport derives from its dependence on elegant gibberish. And of course it remains the author's permanent duty to unbox the lexicon for all eyes to see—a cryptic ticking mechanism in search of a revolution.

The references to the metaphorical association of football and war are especially appropriate. Whereas the traditional mythology of football saw it as a set of heroic actions modeled on warfare, DeLillo has turned the figure upside down. In *End Zone*, war is modeled on football. In Part One, the players for about a week during the preseason play a preadolescent game of Bang You're Dead, which "beneath its bluntness" becomes a "compellingly intricate" thing with "gradations, dark joys, a resonance echoing from the most perplexing of dreams." Thus, the ritualizing and mythologizing of elemental life-and-death combat. A matching piece in Part Three is an informal football game played in the snow. It changes from touch to tackle, and gradually new rules are imposed—no warming of hands, no huddles (plays to be announced), no passing, no reverses—until, ironically, the rules trip away the conventional and ritualistic aspects of the game and it becomes an elemental hand-to-hand struggle. Thus, the civilizing process is reversed.

Gary Harkness is auditing an ROTC course in aspects of modern war, and his dialogues with Major Staley provide the important development of this major theme. Staley believes that future wars will be humane, that is, like games—with rules and conventions like a limit to the megatons each side can use, and clean bombs, and no bombing of cities—just a play of counterforces. Later they play a "crude form of war game" in which only twelve moves complete the game although it takes over three hours. The major points out that the flaw in war games is that they cannot simulate reality because the players are always aware of the game context, but Gary's attitude is captured in the sentence, "Mythic images raged in my mind."

In this remythologizing text, football is constantly giving way to considerations of the largest social, political, and philosophical issues. Most important for this discussion, beyond the still-present stereotypes of animal noises and mindless behavior we can find a football player, like Whitehead's Joiner, who is a cerebral, self-aware, unself-concerned critic of contemporary life. He sees his sport and his fellow athletes as model and symbols of a complex, pluralistic society. On the Logos team are a mystic animist, an expert in economic theory, a mathematical theorist, and a genius who having mastered the knowable is studying the unknowable. There is Bloomberg, a 300-bound speculator in history and the future, who had come to Logos to "unjew" himself. And there is Taft Robinson, the first and only black, who believes in "static forms of beauty" and constructs a complex, if paranoiac, ceremonial existence out of a life consciously reduced to simplicity. It should not be difficult to see that the media's hyping of football players like Namath, Karras, Simpson, and Meredith into contemporary personae is a pale reflection and attenuation of the larger literary movement.

It would be a mistake of even greater proportions to suppose that the cultic attitude is limited to football and its personages. Looking back to *The Great Gatsby* once again as a basic chart of American attitudes in the first part of this century, we find what amounts to a cult of all sports. Gatsby himself, fashioning the pattern of his success, included fifteen minutes of "dumbbell exercise and wall-scaling" at the beginning of his crowded daily schedule and left a half hour in the afternoon for "baseball and sports." Having scaled every wall but one toward his dream, Gatsby has had his picture taken at Oxford with a cricket bat in his hand, introduces Tom Buchanan as "the polo player," and says to Nick about Jordan, "Miss Baker's a great sportswoman, you know, and she'd never do anything that wasn't all right."

Carraway, of course, lacks Gatsby's pure naïveté of attitude. He has heard rumors about Jordan, how at her first big tournament she "had moved her ball from a bad lie in the semi-final round." But Nick, too, is a devotee of the cult. He casts an aura of glamor and elegance around women in terms of sport:

> there was a jauntiness about her movements as if she had first learned to walk upon golf courses on clean, crisp mornings

> all I could think of was how, when that certain girl played tennis, a faint mustache of perspiration appeared on her upper lip

her voice came over the wire as something fresh and cool, as if a divot from a green golf-links had come sailing in at the office window.

Most instructive for our purposes is Nick's reaction to "the man who fixed the World Series in 1919," Meyer Wolfsheim: "It never occurred to me that one man could start to play with the faith of fifty million people." It would never occur to Fitzgerald to question the faith of fifty million Americans in sports, particularly baseball. Even though, as Doctorow demonstrates in *Ragtime*, baseball had already become by the turn of the century the game for waves of immigrant ethnics, it remained in its conception on a mythic level the game of pastoral America.

The baseball myth is carried on in such books as Roger Angell's *Summer Game* and Roger Kahn's *Boys of Summer*, while no spate of Babe Ruth biographies, *Ball Fours*, or *Long Seasons* can dissipate it. Mark Harris's *Bang the Drum Slowly*, brilliantly realized on screen by John Hancock (who also directed the short gem "Sticky My Fingers, Fleet My Feet" from the Tom Meehan story), has enriched the devotional literature, just as *Damn Yankees* extended it to the classic repertory of American musical theater. More important, Bernard Malamud's *The Natural* confronts directly the mythic capacity of the game and Philip Roth's *Great American Novel* plays with it in his most completely realized comedy, while Robert Coover's *The Universal Baseball Association, J. Henry Waugh, Prop.* (discussed briefly in Chapter V) takes baseball's unworldliness and projects it into a symbolic model of an artistically created world.

Common to all the works I have mentioned is an assumption the writer shares with his audience, the society at large, that sports present a coherent world and set of values that we all understand and embrace. Heroes are ready to hand and expected under such conditions, whether they are swallowed whole on the level of myth or taken ironically in relation to a "real world." This and much of what I have been talking about in this chapter are explored in depth in two major novels by John Updike, *Rabbit, Run* (1960) and *Rabbit Redux* (1971).

Harry Angstrom, a former high school basketball star, is Updike's protagonist, but the awareness of sport extends far beyond the game of basketball. In fact, Rabbit's impressions of baseball offer as good a vignette of the game's mythos as I know:

> The spaced dance of the men in white fails to enchant, the code beneath the staccato spurts of distant motion refuses to yield its meaning. Though basketball was his sport, Rabbit remembers the grandeur of all that grass, the excited perilous feeling when a high fly was hoisted your way, the homing-in on the expanding dot, the leathery smack of the catch, the formalized nonchalance of the heads-down trot in toward the bench, the ritual flips and shrugs and the nervous courtesies of the batter's box. There was a beauty here bigger than the hurtling beauty of basketball, a beauty refined from country pastures, a game of solitariness, of waiting, waiting for the pitcher to complete his gaze toward first base and throw his lightning, a game whose very taste, of spit and dust and grass and sweat and leather and sun, was America. . . . Rabbit waits for this beauty to rise to him, through the cheers and the rhythm of innings, the traditional national magic, tasting of his youth; but something is wrong. . . . Rabbit yearns to protect the game from the crowd; the poetry of space and inaction is too fine, too slowly spun for them. And for the players themselves, they seem expert listlessly, each intent on a private dream of making it, making it into the big leagues and the big money, the own-your-own-bowling-alley money, they seem specialists like any other, not men playing a game because all men are boys time is trying to outsmart. A gallant pretense has been abandoned, a delicate balance is being crushed. Only the explosions of orange felt on their uniforms, under the script *Blasts*, evoke the old world of heraldic local loyalties.

Updike takes the familiar theme, the problem of what an athlete does when he doesn't die young, and treats it generally— rather than specially—but profoundly:

You climb up through the little grades and then get to the top and everybody cheers; with the sweat in your eyebrows you can't see very well and the noise swirls around you and lifts you up, and then you're not forgotten at first, just out, and it feels good and cool and free. You're out, and sort of melt, and keep lifting, until you become like to those kids just one more piece of the sky of adults that hangs over them in the town, a piece that for some queer reason has clouded and visited them. They've not forgotten him; worse, they never heard of him.

"You don't think much of yourself, do you?"
"Once the basketball stopped, I suppose not."

The touch is gone. It's a funny feeling when you get old. The brain sends out the order and the body looks the other way.

He explores the athlete's specialness, his separateness, and his mystical feelings of powers in *self*:

a calm flat world where nothing matters much. The last quarter of a basketball game used to carry him into this world; you ran not as the crowd thought for the sake of the score but for yourself, in a kind of idleness. There was you and sometimes the ball and then the hole, the high perfect hole with its pretty skirt of net. It was you, just you and that fringed ring, and sometimes it stayed away, hard and remote and small. It seemed silly for the crowd to applaud or groan over what you had already felt in your fingers or even in your arms as you braced to shoot or for that matter in your eyes: when he was hot he could see the separate threads wound into the strings looping the hoop.

nothing matters much, and I get this funny feeling I can do anything, just drifting around, passing the ball, and all of a sudden I know, you see, I *know* I can do anything. The second half I take maybe just ten shots, and every one goes right in, not just bounces in, but doesn't touch the rim, like I'm dropping stones down a well.

Trapped in realities of an everyday world, Rabbit can only *run*. Goodhearted, wanting to feel love and loved, it all turns away from him. He seems to need an athletic epiphany, a *click* like Brick Pollitt's alcoholic orgasm. For one instant it happens on a golf course, though he is a novice at the game:

> Very simply he brings the clubhead around his shoulder into it. The sound has a hollowness, a singleness he hadn't heard before. His arms force his head up and his ball is hung way out, lunarly pale against the beautiful black blue of storm clouds, his grandfather's color stretched dense across the east. It recedes along a line straight as a ruler-edge. Stricken; sphere, star, speck. It hesitates, and Rabbit thinks it will die, but he's fooled, for the ball makes this hesitation the ground of a final leap: with a kind of visible sob takes a last bite of space before vanishing in falling. "That's *it!*" he cries and, turning to Eccles with a smile of aggrandizement, repeats, "That's it."

In *Rabbit Redux* he has run further aground. What he knows deeply has receded to distant metaphors as he has become Archie Bunker. Still, "the presence of any game reassures Rabbit. Where any game is being played a hedge exists against fury," he thinks when he finds a pool game going on at Jimbo's, a black bar far outside his familiar world.

In Harry's world, the values have been formulated by people like Coach Tothero, who claims concern with "developing the three tools we are given in life; the head, the body, and the heart." A hero to every emotional tot in his charge, the coach pontificates about "the will to achieve. I've always liked that better than the will to win, for there can be achievement even in defeat . . . the *sacredness* of achievement, in the form of giving our best." Ironically, Tothero's life belies every piety he utters, but his maxim that "a boy who has had his heart enlarged by an inspiring coach can never become, in the deepest sense, a failure in the greater game of life" still rings true for Harry.

The game itself, beyond the strategy and conditioning and elegance that Tothero spiels about, has invested Harry with a mindset, with values, and with a frame of reference. His ex-teammate Ronnie Harrison he puts down because "In the locker room he was always talking about making out and playing with himself under his little hairy pot of a belly and that pot has really grown." But he was a teammate, and so Rabbit "remembers one night when Harrison came back into the game after losing two teeth to somebody's elbow and tries to be glad to see him. There were just five of you out there at one time and the other four for that time were unique in the world." His wife's lover, Stavros, is put down as "a type he never liked, the competitor. The type that sits on the bench doing the loudmouth bit until the coach sends them in with a play or with orders to foul. Brainy cute close-set little playmakers." Their whole confrontation is perceived as a basketball game. Finally, it is partly through basketball that Harry achieves a limited breakthrough to an understanding and sharing with Skeeter, a figure of another generation and race and world, but a mirror image of Rabbit running:

> They scrimmage one on one; Skeeter is quick and slick, slithering by for the layup on the give-and-go to Nelson again and again. Rabbit cannot stop him, his breath begins to ache in his chest, but there are moments when the ball and his muscles and the air overhead and the bodies competing with his all feel taut and unified and defiant of gravity.

Throughout the two novels there is a movement out from sports to the world at large which they illuminate. Most sports fiction moves in the opposite direction, projecting the world of experience into a symbolic arena. A notable exception is Jason Miller's prize-winning play *That Championship Season*, where the characters measure their perceptions of life after sport against the model and values of their basketball triumph years ago. The audience progressively learns that the relationships are all false; the lessons of sport are irrelevant to life; at best the world of experience is a travesty of the sporting model. Then, in the climax, the ideals of the basketball championship are revealed to be false themselves. The nostalgia is mythic—directed back toward a golden age that never was—but it is all the former players and their coach have.

Jason Miller's dramatic construction is reminiscent of the thematic basis of the Rabbit books. Updike, too, has closely approximated the perceptions of a society that sees in sports an ideal model for living—however unrealistic or distorting or itself distorted. Thus, near the end of *Rabbit, Run,* Harry has a "vivid dream":

> He is alone on a large sporting field, or vacant lot, littered with small pebbles. In the sky two perfect disks, identical in size but the one a dense white and the other slightly transparent, move toward each other slowly; the pale one is directly above the dense one. At the moment they touch he feels frightened and a voice like over a loudspeaker at a track meet announces, "The cowslip swallows up the elder." The downward gliding of the top one continues steadily until the other, though the stronger, is totally eclipsed, and just one circle is before his eyes, pale and pure. He understands: "the cowslip" is the moon, and "the elder" the sun, and that what he has witnessed is the explanation of death: lovely life eclipsed by lovely death. With great excitement he realizes he must go forth from this field and found a new religion.

A religion, a Tao, a way of life with its roots in sport is often envisioned or embodied in the way fiction recreates our society and appeals to a mass audience. It seems hardly worth reporting, because so *acceptable* a phenomenon, that the final group playing for the championship of the Bob Hope Desert Classic at Indian Wells in Palm Springs last year consisted of two active Mormons, Johnny Miller and Billy Casper, and the leader of the PGA tour's Bible-study group, Rik Massengale. Strange truth, apparently, is more acceptable than fiction.

Michael Murphy's *Golf in the Kingdom* is so startling a book that it completely fooled the cataloguers at the Library of Congress. As a result, not only on Capitol Hill but all over the country, the novel will be found in the GV collections of libraries—the technical, historical, biographical, analytical, theoretical, polemical, and journalistic books on sports—instead of in the fiction collections where it belongs. The mistake is understandable. A philosophical dialogue, which is what constitutes a substantial portion of the book, often reads unlike fiction, particularly when written in the first person by as well-known a personage as Murphy. First-personage fiction is a rare genre, unless the fanciful celebrity memoir be included.

The name of Murphy's main character, golf pro/guru Shivas Irons, should probably have tipped off the cataloguers, even though Murphy indulges in subtly tongue-in-cheek etymology about the name. But I think what really caused the misclassification was the cultural context into which *Golf in the Kingdom* emerged. Murphy, after all, a founder of Esalen, might well have been expected to share in the movement toward self-awareness in sport, toward transcendent experience in physical activity, and toward the wedding of Eastern philosophy and Western behavior. The remarkable book by George Leonard, *The Ultimate Athlete,* should be read by all those interested in this subject. Actually this movement was but part of a much larger cultural phenomenon discussed in Chapter VII, the efforts to convert a population from a nation of spectators to a nation of participants. This, too, shows up in popular fiction. For example, in William Goldman's *Marathon Man*, the unlikely, unprepossessing, intellectual hero triumphs in the spy-melodrama-thriller for three reasons: first, he is a runner; second, he conjures up the spirits of his heroes—Nurmi and Bikila—to run with him; third, he wills himself through his run to salvation by psyching himself with the cliché proverbs of sports.

I have only scratched the surface here in an attempt to suggest the pervasiveness of sports-mindedness in our literature. For a study of specific themes associated with the subject, I refer the reader to Wiley Lee Umphlett's *The Sporting Myth and the American Experience* (1975). In addition to many of the writers I have cited, Umphlett draws material from classics by Washington Irving, James Fenimore Cooper, Jack London, Sinclair Lewis, Thomas Wolfe, Lardner, Hemingway, and Faulkner, from major contemporary figures like Bellow, Algren, Marquand, Cheever, Wright Morris, Nemerov, Schulberg, J. F. Powers, James Jones, and Caroline Gordon, and from such minor writers as Knowles, Wallop, Neugeboren, Larner, Leonard Gardner, and Owen Johnson.

Even more instructive is the classification achieved by Jack Higgs in his as yet unpublished "Apollo, Dionysius, and Adonis: The Myths of the Athlete in American Literature." In Higgs's comprehensive formulation, the Apollonian athletic types are "those who have stopped growing or if growing are trying to conform to a conception of completeness that they have formulated in their own minds. They are the know-it-alls, the true believers who have panaceas for the dispensation of knowledge, the banishment of evil, and the control of nature. They are unrealistic, immature, though giving the illusion of maturity, and if given enough prominence, tyrannical and oppressive."

He finds ten categories of "Apollo: the Artificial": (1) The Busher, with examples from Lardner and Runyon; (2) The Leisure-Class Gentleman, from Fitzgerald and Hemingway; (3) The Southern Knight, from Thomas Wolfe; (4) The Apotheosized Wasp, from O'Neill; (5) The Student Athlete, from Thurber, O'Neill, and Jenkins; (6) The Booster Alumnus, from Anderson, Thurber, and Roth; (7) The Christian Athlete, from Lewis; (8) The Golden Boy, from Odets; (9) The Modern Ephebus, from Inge; and (10) The Brave New Man, from Albee.

The Dionysian type, on the other hand, is the true natural "who has accepted his body as himself and feels no need to conform to an Apollonian order of any sort. He is, in fact, narcissistic in that he worships his own body as an end in itself. He seeks not to become at all." A trinity of categories is discovered here: (1) The Babe, from London and Schulberg; (2) The Bum, from Warren and Inge; and (3) The Beast, from Lardner and Jenkins.

Finally, the Adonis type is

> genuinely heroic. He is heroic in that he is an eternal rebel who reminds us of greater beyonds. . . . He does not kill himself . . .

nor uncritically conform. Invariably he is a sacrificial figure. He is the familiar *pharmakos* who is eternally persecuted by Apollo. He is "natural" man, in one sense, but never so natural, unlike Dionysius, that he does not seek transcendence in some way. Like Adonis himself, he is a divided being who reminds us that while body and self must be united, no man or group can ever say with certainty what the highest quality of that synthesis is. As in the classical myths, Adonis defies both authority *and* nature. He will not conform to temporal goals nor merge in dionysian fashion with the all. He lives in a world of eternal tension, of endless pain, struggle, and hope. Whatever reality is, Adonis reminds us that it is not the partialized decrees of Apollo nor the mindless merging of Dionysius. He is eternally persecuted because he either cannot or will not accept the world's stereotyped definitions of what it means to be a man.

Higgs has isolated five categories of "Adonis: The Heroic": (1) The Folk Hero, from London, Wolfe, Malamud, Harris, and Runyon; (2) The Fisher King, from Williams; (3) The Scapegoat, from Cheever and Wright Morris; (4) The Absurd Athlete, from Farrell, Updike, and Faulkner; and (5) The "Secret" Christian, from Anderson, Auchincloss, and Whitehead.

There remain a couple of observations that extend the views of this chapter toward the subject of the next. For one thing, we should note that literary figures of our time often strive to associate with athletes. Norman Mailer wasn't alone in following Muhammad Ali to Zaire. Hunter S. Thompson was there, and Budd Schulberg, and the ubiquitous dabbler George Plimpton (enough, as John Leonard observed, "to bake a Bhagavad-Gita"). The point is that the athletes are at the center of the action, in the center ring where most public attention is focused, and like politicians and other entertainers the artists swirl about this focal point of celebrity making. The jocks are the personages; contact with them aids in the creation of media personalities.

For another, we need to see the boundaries of literature being pushed out to embrace the mass media. As pervasive as sports are in the substance, texture, and framework of written narrative, they are even more influential in the fictions of movies, television, and comic strips. The most casual glance at these forms should register their preoccupation with sports. Here too the three phases of mythologizing, demythologizing, and re-mythologizing exist simultaneously. On the same page, for example, one may find crew-cut Gil Thorpe applying the ancient verities of sport to his contemporary social problems, the on-target satire of "Tank McNamara" shooting holes in all the pious traditions of the norts spews, and a primitive attempt to encompass a contemporary sports ethic in the unlikely figure of Milton Caniff's Stalky Schweisenberg. In the mass media is found probably the clearest evidence that, in our jockocracy, the crowns of the laureate are comfortably worn only if ivy is prominently wreathed in among the laurel.

# IV

## TEN CENTS
## A DANCE

The athlete is the high-priced whore of our society. He sells his body for the pleasure of others, as and when they want it, and no matter what his salary is the real profit goes to the promoters, the franchise dealers, the "owners" who act as his pimps. The widespread notion of the athlete as a mindless performer reinforces this image, so that the curious anomaly of the "articulate athlete" has become as much of a cliché as the "whore with a heart of gold." In the vernacular of the sixties this chapter would be called "The Athlete as Nigger," but the idea remains the same. The society as a whole conspires to maintain the system of exploitation while it rationalizes away any sense of being exploiters in the false perception that "successful" athletes are far from being exploited.

But that's show biz. The tritest cliché of all has become the most appropriate. Virtually every time we hear the conventional wisdom that sports are big business, we also hear that it is just part of the show business. When collegiate athletic directors talk about budgetary problems, they are more likely to say something about being "in competition for the entertainment dollar" than to talk about the way that education appropriations are divided. Proprietors of professional sports facilities talk in terms of booking events, and they are equally comfortable with athletic events or circuses or rock concerts in their houses.

Media moguls talk of sports in terms of prime-time programming, and the popular conception of sporting events as escape from the real world is prevalent even in serious philosophical discussions of the subject. Athletes, when successful and colorful, become instant media personalities, and then they are bought and sold for more than their bodies: their "integrity" is put on the line or the block as they become shills for products and services and industries.

It becomes quite clear in any analysis that there are many roles and functions of sport in our society. Yet the perception that it is first and foremost a vital part of the entertainment business is what governs much of the thinking of those people who play active leadership roles in sport. Moreover, they are most comfortable with a popular public perception that sports are *no more* than entertainment or pleasure, a way of satisfying the public need for ways to occupy ever-increasing leisure time.

In class I discussed issues of role and function on separate occasions with several of my guests. One was Peter O'Malley, the bright and able politician and attorney who has become president of the Washington Capitals. Talking about violence in hockey, he was careful to distinguish between the bullying that everyone abhors and the violent action that is part of the game. He said,

> The nature of the sport is to be the most physical and the fastest moving of all sports, in my judgment. It's an entertainment form, as is every sport. Its appeal is to the fan that pays the dollar, and the large majority come to see the physical aspects of it, not a stick to the head but two players colliding at rapid speed or two men going into the boards.

In another connection, and wearing another of his many hats as a regent of the University of Maryland, the versatile O'Malley said that he was not uncomfortable with the practical operations of big-time university athletics as farm systems for certain professional sports, though he didn't see that as the primary purpose of college sports. "Athletics is entertainment and professional sport is entertainment," he reaffirmed. "And collegiate athletes who have the requisite skills naturally progress."

O'Malley is persuasive as much by his disarming directness and absence of rhetoric as by his quick grasp of practical considerations. But what makes me uncomfortable about his line of reasoning is that the sports-as-entertainment proposition operates in a closed circle defined, described, and determined by the premise that the appeal to the dollar is basic and in the end the dollar will be decisive. This may be true, insofar as it operates in the system, insofar as the men who operate the system look no further than this bottom (if circular) line. But I would suggest a need to look further, to the philosophical implications of this whole position.

I explored these issues from another angle and in greater depth with Don V. Ruck, vice-president of the National Hockey League and president of National Hockey League Services. Ruck came to his job with an ideal set of qualifications. Aside from personal qualities of the kind of quiet authoritativeness that inspires confidence and an understated wit and style, he had a decade's experience as a sportswriter and more than a decade's experience in marketing with a genuine bent for market research. One of his primary charges was to market hockey as a viable television commodity, and he continues to wrestle with the problems of promoting NHL hockey on TV when it may be too fast a game for an audience largely unfamiliar with it to follow. His market research teaches him that educating a larger audience is a key to higher ratings.

Moving obliquely toward the point that sports are influenced to their own detriment by considerations of commerce and mass media, I asked him, "How did the network television contract interact with plans for expansion in 1967 and then later?"

He responded directly:

Exposure is essential, whatever the business. We doubled our business in the 1967–1968 season. We moved into markets where hockey is not indigenous to this country, including Los Angeles and San Francisco. To sell the product, which is entertainment—that's the business we are in—we needed television exposure for the obvious reasons that one telecast beamed across a network will reach more people than perhaps the combined circulation of all the newspapers in those cities could reach in a month.

Everything ties in to the marketing concept: build a larger base for the acceptance of the product; multiply sales and profits.

Later, I asked him about the question of blacking out TV coverage for home games, whether sold out or not. He answered, in part,

When *My Fair Lady* broke on Broadway, it cost at that time nine or ten dollars to get a ticket. But you couldn't buy a ticket for two years. I wanted to see it, but couldn't get a ticket. I wasn't born with a God-given right to see *My Fair Lady*, not when some other guy put his money into it, produced it, took all the losses if there were going to be any. I could buy a ticket like anyone else. For a year and a half I couldn't get a ticket. I didn't go running down to Congress; I didn't call up Bella Abzug.

Our position is simply that the team owners are the people who have their dollars in the business, the investments have been put in by our people, like *any other business*. And like any other business, your rights under the Constitution should be fair and equal, and that should mean, it seems to me, that we should have the right to control the manner in which we sell our entertainment. To me there is a severe question of a breach of the Constitution in the existing blackout bill that forces a person to handle his product in a way that he does not voluntarily elect to do.

He went on to point out that, for its own reasons, its own marketing decisions, the NHL did not, as a rule, black out a telecast of a game in the home team's city. But the league is opposed to any rule or law that "means that the decision is taken out of the hands of the man who owns the business."

It is interesting that for all the talk about entertainment business, marketing concepts, and parity under the law with any other business, there is an entirely different story concerning the special nature of the hockey business. Like baseball, hockey has enormous expenses in farm systems to develop players and therefore should be exempted like baseball from the antitrust restrictions for any other business. To give due credit, the NHL has handled these complex matters perhaps better than any other sport. It achieved with the players a Collective Bargaining Agreement wherein the players themselves recognize a team's right to compensation if a team loses a player when the player becomes a free agent.

Don Ruck is, I think, most eloquent when he talks about another uniqueness of his business that sets it apart from all other businesses. The board of governors of the National Hockey League sits as an entity, acting to form a consensus on issues, policies, and rules in the best interests of the organization. But as soon as that meeting is over, every team goes on about its business of trying to beat every other team. The ultimate tensiveness of absolute competition within a closed and therefore unified system is the integrity of the game. And this integrity, which Don Ruck and many others cherish, is what I fear may be lost if the entertainment-business label is accepted as the be-all and end-all of all sports.

When I talked of these fears with Abe Pollin, owner of the Capital Centre, the Washington Bullets, and the Washington Capitals, I found that he didn't share them because his own integrity operates to dispel them. In the small, exclusive club of professional sports owners, Pollin is a clear exception to the general notions with which I began this chapter. Sports for him are an abiding love, but not a hobby; sports business for him is a full-time occupation, but neither a way to quick profit nor a way to take tax write-offs against the profits of other businesses. He has built and owns the place where his teams play, the Capital Centre. Pollin treats players as people, not property, and this too, along with his reputation for probity and straightforwardness, makes him a smallest minority of a tiny minority.

I asked him about his show business involvement brought about by his building the house that is his teams' home:

> You're now involved in a lot of things that are only indirectly and sometimes not at all associated with sports. How do you feel about that?
>
> It's a very exciting part of the business.

He said that in 1975 there were 265 total events at the Capital Centre, that there would be around 300 in 1976, but that sporting events would not add up to more than 100.

> Are sports now just part of the entertainment business as a whole? Do you think in terms of promoting your athletic teams in competition with other opportunities for spending the entertainment dollar?
>
> Sure, we're changing hats all day long. One minute we're in the circus business, the next it's an ice show.

I tried to suggest to him that this delightful variety of activities could have deleterious implications for sports:

> What concerns me are values and attitudes. If the promoter is producing events that are pure entertainment (rock concerts, circuses), events that are quasi-sports entertainments (featuring Andre the Giant and Bruno Sanmartino), and also producing events that feature people like Bill Walton and Elvin Hayes, who had a fascinating confrontation last week, what does that do to the attitude toward sports? Are they just another kind of exhibition, just another kind of show? Are the Waltons and the Hayeses entertainers like Andre the Giant and JoJo Starbuck?

His answer was both intelligent and innocent:

> It's a question of definition. You have to buy tickets for them all, and in that sense they're the same. They're all separate and distinct,

but still they are all competing for the entertainment dollar. The
Bullets or Capitals playing a game aren't in the same league with the
Harlem Globetrotters, for example, but they compete for the same
potential audience.

In the wholesomeness of his own attitudes, Abe Pollin can be con-
fident that the vital distinctions will be properly made. Others cannot be so sanguine, because we suspect and fear that there aren't
enough Abe Pollins in positions of power and influence.

I discussed some of the same issues with Jerry Sachs, Pollin's
second in command as president of the Capital Centre and executive vice-president of the Washington Bullets, a personable executive whose soft-spoken manner does not disguise the sophisticated
intelligence he brings to bear on these matters. I asked him if he
was at all uncomfortable after a career in sports management with
being in show business, promoting rock concerts and the like.
"No," he said. "It's fun."

Then came my standard question: "Is the function of professional sports, then, strictly entertainment?"

His answer was, in part, a frank, pragmatic version of what
Pollin has said:

> We could not have built the Capital Centre without knowing that
> we would have events other than about a hundred athletic events. In
> actual fact, we hope to have three hundred or more events, so you
> can see that sports occupy just one third of the total number of
> events. In order to make it viable economically we had to make cer-
> tain that it was built to accommodate events other than basketball,
> hockey, and box lacrosse.
>
> A large percentage of professional sports should be classified as en-
> tertainment. I don't have a precise figure but I believe that the con-
> cept of professional athletics is one that is primarily involved in enter-
> tainment.

This raised more questions than it answered. Would this large
percentage of professional sports be reduced to a common classification with professional wrestling? I was reminded of the era of

big-money TV quiz games, when the producers' defense, after the scandalous revelations that the contestants were given answers in advance, was that they were in the entertainment business and were guaranteeing more exciting entertainment for their audiences. Where do you draw the line between applying the standards of entertainment and the standards of competitive sport? Isn't there a tendency to corrupt sport when honest competition is sacrificed to audience demands?

Sachs's answer implied a subtle relativism that is the pragmatist's version of situation ethics: "The line changes with changes in our culture." He reminisced about his background in professional baseball, a "lethargic, antiquated sport mired in tradition" but in which such changes as new uniform design and World Series games at night have come about with entertainment thinking without seriously undercutting the game's integrity. He said that the people who are in policy-making positions had to be careful not to destroy what they had by catering to current tastes. By way of parable, he told about the two versions of roller derby, with the jazzed-up spectacle forcing out the honest competition, only to lose in the long run much of the audience appeal that had apparently determined the issue. The more volatile the fad the more easily jaded the faddist fans.

"But the line," I said, "is drawn by people you'd not necessarily want to draw it, people outside sport, media people. Television in particular has a great deal to say about changes in sports to suit programming concepts."

"It all goes back to the almighty dollar," he said.

From a pragmatic point of view, when we talk about sports as entertainment business, we are talking finally less about what works to entertain than about what works to show a profit. The bottom line is the business, not the entertainment. Thus the role of sports in occupying ever-increasing leisure time becomes a function of providing means for successful commercial enterprise. And the athlete? He gets paid, often very well, for doing his tricks, but his skill and his image are just scrip in the system's transactions.

The "civilizing functions of sport" is a phrase used in two distinct senses. One, an idea developed by J. Huizinga in *Homo Ludens*, is that sports and games are both measures and actual vehicles of societies' development, by their imposition of orderly patterns, abstract principles, and controlled behavior. The other is that participation in sports, either active by playing or by proxy in rooting, is a way to involve people in their society, get them to embrace the civilization of their time and place. In either sense, sports act as a conservative element in society.

Success in sports means attaining status in the status quo. Arising from the imposition of rules, structures, and orderly procedures, sports are nurtured in the rigid maintenance of things as they are and have always been. Elaborate bureaucratic superstructures are erected to define, codify, regulate, legislate, and chronicle those things and to keep things that way. In time, the function of the bureaucracy becomes, as always, to maintain itself, which is seen as the way to maintain the game.

It is with an essential irony, then, that a discussion of the role and function of sports in our society turns to the notion of sport as a vehicle for social change. I am not talking here about sport as a vehicle for upward social mobility, the way to acceptance and assimilation that immigrant minorities found mostly in baseball, football, and basketball; I am not talking about sport as a way out of the ghetto. These are ways of strengthening the status quo, ways by which a few get to share the perqs of the establishment. These are false hopes held to the masses, because only a very few fulfill the hopes while the masses are repressed in their unsuccessful attempts while at the same time diverted from potentially successful, explosive, perhaps revolutionary vehicles.

No, what I am talking about is the use of sports as models for social progress in such areas as racial and sexual equality. The capacity is there, for example, in the way a group of men from diverse backgrounds can become a closely knit herd, concerned with the welfare of all, transcending all social distinctions. I am reminded of the delighted glee with which John Lucas has talked about traveling with the University of Maryland tennis team: "We had two New Zealanders, a Venezuelan, a black from North Carolina, one straight Anglo, and one hippy." But the successfully integrated teams that cut across the lines of social distinctions are rare, and the notion of sports as a great melting pot is largely an illusion. Because of the conservative nature of sports establishments, social change is rigorously resisted in sports and the stereotyping of athletic roles persists.

David DuPree, sportswriter for the *Washington Post*, illustrated racist stereotyping in football with a story from his undergraduate days at the University of Washington in Seattle. They had recruited an outstanding high school quarterback for the Huskies; the coaches had never met him, though they had seen him in action and on film, and did not know he was a light-skinned black. "On the first day, you get your equipment and then you go out on the field where you're listed by number and position for the freshman team. When he walked on the field he was the number one quarterback, but when they saw him without his helmet on he became a third-string defensive back."

Roy Jefferson, Washington Redskins wide receiver, echoed this point in telling about his own experience as a pro. He had played end, on both offense and defense, at the University of Utah and was All-American in his senior year. But he was drafted as a defensive back. The shift to wide receiver came midway through his first year as a Pittsburgh Steeler:

> They kept bouncing me back and forth between offense and defense. They tried every clown on the team as a wide receiver. None of them lasted more than a year or two. This is part of the racial problems that still exist in professional football. I was the starting wide receiver at the end of the exhibition season. And the first home game, first game of the season, they were announcing the starters before the game and they were getting ready to announce the wide receiver. I'm standing there ready to go, a hotdog to my heart, thinking about how I'm going to run out there . . . and then they announce Red Mack as the starter. He'd bounced around from Pittsburgh to other teams and to Canada and had just been picked up by Pittsburgh again a week ear-

lier. He'd been in camp for four days and he was announced as starting wide receiver. And I couldn't deal with that, couldn't understand
it. I took it as a racial slur.

Jefferson, who grew up in Los Angeles, had only recently come to
some racial awareness. After almost "four fine years—no problems—at Utah" he wanted to spend his last six months living in
some style for a change. He had his bonus from Pittsburgh, he had
a wife and a new baby, and he wanted to live in a decent apart-
ment. But prospective landlords, including two Mormon bishops,
said they'd have to raise the rent $10 a month for a six-month lease.
Feeling free and easy with some real money in the bank for the
first time in his life, he agreed and even offered to pay for the
whole six months in advance. But then he was told that six-month
leases would not be allowed anyway. From that point on, he has
been quick to see the issue of race in any situation that suggests
discrimination in even the subtlest ways.

In discussing the matter of stereotyping, DuPree told the
class that black high school football centers will be converted to
tackles in college because guards are still too close to the ball, and
that the process is repeated in the pros wherever it has not already
taken place in college. Jefferson's experience substantiates this
along with the further observations that the outstanding players
will do all right at their chosen positions, that marginal players are
more likely to hang on if they are white, and that among the whites
the ones who take orders and fit in best are more likely to hang on
in marginal roles.

DuPree extended the view to coaches, managers, executives,
and even writers. He noted that the *Post*, under some pressures
from a variety of sources, internal and external, had to reach all the
way to San Francisco to hire him from the *Wall Street Journal*.
And he remembered his first trip to cover a Super Bowl where out
of 600 reporters only nine were black and six of those were with
black newspapers. The point is that even in the sporting world,
where black Americans have had their most conspicuous success

(outside of a few other specialized areas of the show business), the establishment has kept them in their place and out of the establishment.

Race is thus only the most visible version of the essential "them and us" structure of sports. Roy Jefferson's experience, for example, translates the black/white dichotomy into labor/management. His trade from Pittsburgh to the Baltimore Colts, he said, "stemmed from my being the player representative. Rooney said that had it not been for me his team would have come into camp in our first strike in 1968." He told of an incident that illustrates the frustration he feels in the struggle of what seems like common humanity versus inhuman power structure.

It was an extraordinarily hot and humid day in training camp and the Steeler coaches were drilling the players, particularly rookies, with the exuberant zeal of Marine sergeants in boot camp. There were only two wide receivers available for the practice because of a variety of injuries and other excuses, but the coaches dictated one more passing drill than seemed reasonable. A rookie, Hubie Grimes, became dehydrated and passed out. In the dressing room, where this compliant rookie hovered near death briefly, the sweat was popping off his body in bullet-sized beads and Jefferson, standing nearby, was struck by one. At this point, his objections as player representative to management abuses escalated into a tearful, emotional outburst.

Grimes recovered but he didn't stick with the team. Jefferson left camp, troubled and upset, not really in control of himself and frustrated at the players' total lack of control over the situation of training practices. For his humanity Jefferson was labeled a trouble-maker. That kind of humanity, that fellow-feeling that is often thought to be a positive value and goal of sports, is dangerous because it threatens to make trouble for the coaches, the management, the system.

The focus of attention has shifted recently from issues of racism in sport to issues of sexism. The women's movement turned its energies to inequities in the sporting world almost as an afterthought. Perhaps this was because there already were well-established traditions of women's golf and women's tennis, perhaps because of the high incidence of lesbianism in those two groups, or perhaps because to the movement the sporting world seemed insufficiently serious an arena.

Yet in hindsight it appears to have been a particularly offensive bastion of all kinds of chauvinism and sexist most of all. Long considered the special domain of the male, sports have only recently opened up to the point of welcoming women as spectators, never mind participants. The most egregiously sexist attitudes are those of football-minded coaches and sportswriters who taunt players with being girls or pussies for any kind of weakness. When superb athletes came along who happened to be women, like Babe Didrikson and Althea Gibson, jokes were commonly made about their masculinity. These jokes persist with reference to women's track and field athletes, particularly the champion performers from East Germany, Bulgaria, and the USSR. Now the issue of sex tests has been drawn between gynecological legalists versus genetic chromosomists, with a splinter group of hormone- level counters attacking both parties.

It is as if after all this time we are still at the point of confusing gender with sex and both with specific traits. And we still seem to accept the primitive notion that there are just two polar opposites, male and female, period. Don't let the jokes fool you. Feelings run very deep on these issues. The word "jock" itself is enough to cause a furor, even if used in perfect innocence to mean merely "athlete" or "sports" as I use it in my title, as I discovered in Vermillion, South Dakota, where I was bitterly denounced by a radical lesbian linguist, who couldn't even bring herself to hear what I was saying in my talk, so incensed was she over the sexist connotations of that word.

By now, however, significant strides have been taken in sports to bring about some general public awareness of the inequalities between the sexes that are harbored in our society. Billie Jean Moffitt King, who could have been sufficiently admirable for her tennis game and her fierce competitiveness that made her the best in the world, became a genuine culture hero by smashing away at the arbitrary inequities between men's and women's tennis and by demolishing some of the deepest male prejudices against abortion. When girls began to make inroads into the precociously sexist world of Little League sports, men made the issue ridiculous in the popular perception by going to great lengths to keep them out. The warm reception for a movie such as *Bad News Bears* indicates a broad acceptance of the premise that a girl can be an outstanding pitcher. In other sports, such as archery and shooting, women have shown they can be competitive with men. In horse racing and automobile racing, the resistance to women has made the men appear in many people's perception to be malicious little boys. And in some areas, like marathon swimming, a performer like Diana Nyad has reminded us all over again that women may be athletically superior to men.

In many ways, however, the sports establishment has effectively shown its reluctance to be used as a vehicle for social change, as much on issues of sex discrimination as on any other. For a period of about two years, for example, the NCAA, with its formidable lobbying power, held up passage of Title IX, arguing primarily (and speciously) that enactment would cause undue financial hardships. Finally passed into law, the bill calls for equality of opportunity for men and women alike. The problems really begin at the point of passage, with the issues of implementation and affirmative action passed along to the very people who opposed Title IX most vigorously.

I discussed these matters in class with Dorothy McKnight, who for eleven years at the University of Maryland served the cause of equality for the sexes from her position as teacher and coach. She supported Title IX and then resigned from the university, where she was director of women's athletics, because she couldn't live with the decisions on implementation. "Everyone assumes," she said, "that equality must come from the women giving up what they want, so that they can have and do what the men have and do." She expressed her great disappointment that the university, which could have taken the initiative and played a role of leadership for change in intercollegiate athletics, instead took the easiest way out.

McKnight believes in the opportunity for athletic activity for all. She also believes that no program is complete without both intercollegiate and intramural activities. To this end she believes that the institutions themselves should support these activities. But she supports the idea of talent grants as rewards for deserving students to be used at any institution as opposed to athletic scholarships awarded on a contractual basis of *quid pro quo*, which she considers, by definition, professionalism.

She talked about "King Football" and "Prince Basketball"— the big, revenue-producing sports—as diverting attention from the needed areas of large-scale student involvement. Now, as affirmative action, the university proposes to annoint a "Queen Basketball" and "Princess Volleyball." In her view, this simply recapitulates the mistakes of men's sports, where the recruiting practices and granting of scholarships move the emphasis away from the needs of individual students and places it upon "the needs of institutions and the desires of coaches." This is what she couldn't live with, because the spirit of Title IX is thereby thwarted. Instead of equal opportunity for all women and men, this implementation perpetuates the special privileges for a select few, presumably in the best interests of the institution. One of those interests would seem to be the *appearance* of compliance with the law, in addition to the characteristic impulse to re-entrench the establishment itself. "In reality," McKnight has written, "this implementation which finds women's programs placed in the same model and pattern as men's is even more discriminatory for it takes from women in athletics the precious right to determine the direction of their programs—a right which men have experienced since the inception of intercollegiate athletics."

In all these examples, then, the role and function of sports in the area of social change may be perceived as giving the illusion of constructive change while actually obstructing change in the defense of established orders. One is reminded inevitably of the argument that in the interests of national security illegal acts may be committed against the freedoms of some in order to protect the freedom of all. What is really protected is the power of the established authority. And on both sides of the analogy, the individual participants are merely used at the pleasure and for the purpose of the power structure.

Now behind all these subject-oriented arguments, behind these identifications of content in sports' roles and functions in society, stands the *structure* of competition. And it is here, perhaps, that we find the most significant aspect of sport. The abstract and arbitrary division of groups into polar parties constitutes a way of organizing societies and channeling potentially dangerous, divisive, destructive forces into a supportive and systematic order. Whatever their origins may have been, we know that the division of tribes into moieties or into totemic groupings has consistently been an effective means of maintaining the unity and integrity of whole societies.

The traditional color war at summer camps illustrates the working of such a structure. In these events the entire camp community is divided into two teams which then compete in every conceivable way for a set number of days. There are athletic events, contests of intellectual games, competitions in the performance of songs and skits, and scoring of such modes of behavior as neatness and orderly movement between activities and even proper dining procedures. The idea is to keep the competition as close as possible, spirits as high as possible, and rivalry as fierce as possible. The placing of particularly close friends on the same side is avoided generally, and each individual is given the sense of contributing to his side in some point-worthy way. When it's all over, the camp reunites in a healthy, loyal whole.

Sports function as a kind of mass proxy color war for the American people. Super Bowls and World Series get us all choosing up sides and entering as a whole into a ritual activity that unites us in a healthy, tensive, vital, structural oneness. On a smaller scale, every sports event plays the same sort of role, and our society as a whole embraces the very idea of competition as an ideological bulwark. This structural argument is not briefly offered here to be tested for validity, but only to suggest another dimension to the problems of role and function posed in this chapter. But before we turn in the following chapter to the dysfunctions and malfunctions, before we examine the erosion of values and misdirections in those roles, let me offer one final caveat here. Let the perception of the structural contributions of the jockocracy not obscure our perceptions of the jocks themselves. Offered to us, at a price, for our pleasure, they serve not an abstract idea of structure but a concrete, rigid, established power structure.

# WITHERED
# GARLANDS

The individual participating in sports is supposed to reap a beneficial harvest in such virtues or values as cooperation and fair play, the control of destructive behavior, immediate rewards for performance, and alleviation of pressures and frustrations. Veblen reminds us that self-reliance and good-fellowship, two of the qualities most often stressed by sports apologists, may simply be masks for truculence and clannishness. For athletes, every positive trait may be subverted by the practices of their sport, every civilizing process may be transformed to antisocial behavior. For spectators, who would have difficulty constructing an ethical imperative out of their fandom in the first place, contemporary sports breed a wholesale corruption of values.

In general, three distinct but interrelated transvaluations occur in the process by which positive sports values are subverted: the value of the game itself becomes less important than the winning of the game; the value of playing a game to win becomes confused with the profit motive; and the value of organization for the sake of the game becomes less important than the drive to strengthen the system of organization for its own sake. I can think of no clearer demonstration of the whole degenerative process than the 1976 Olympics in Montreal. Many of the following observations were included in reports I made to the *Washington Post*, particularly in one article that was headlined, "Rx for Olympics; Leave Flags Home, Return Games to Athletes."

The Olympic Games should be the pinnacle of athletic competition, but in many ways they are not. For the fans, the spectacle and excitement are there, but the Games are not run for the sake of the athletes or the sports. Few of the spectators understand this, and perhaps fewer care.

Every event attracts fans who care about the particular sport, aficionados who applaud the right things and make the appropriate comments and decry the bum decisions. But just as many are there simply because it's an Olympic event—people who say "Which one is Kupchack?" or "The program says 'pentathlon,' but the girls are high-jumping."

This is no different from other major sporting events. All are tourist attractions and there is a kind of social satisfaction, a status thing, with having been there. [Like other tourist attractions of sports, the Olympics capitalize on this aspect by a massive inundation of souvenirs for sale. But beyond the typical commercialization,] the Olympics take fans on an emotional binge that detracts from the Games, and the athletes themselves must suffer the distractions and detractions.

The Olympics should be taken away from the promoters, executives, committees, concessionaires, and other parasites whose primary function is to feed their own self-interest and who only secondarily serve the Games. The Olympics should be given back to the athletes.

I used to think a fair amount of ignorance and some stupidity were involved in the way the athletic competition of the Games was subordinated to their spectacle, ceremonial, and nationalistic aspects, but I have come to understand that all this is largely a product of bureaucratic canniness.

It is entirely in the paramilitary and show-biz-production-number dimensions of the Olympics that the non-athletes gain ascendancy and control over the athletes. To a degree this is true of most organized sports, but it has never been more apparent than in Montreal.

It seemed a lack of intelligence or understanding that made people think the Olympic Games needed a constant hyping of ballyhoo and pomp and circumstance—that the athletic competitions themselves would not attract the audience.

Setting aside the question of whether the athletes would be satisfied to prove themselves in competition against the world's best without an audience, I now think the functionaries and flunkies have always known the great attraction for fans of athletic competition at the highest level and have labored diligently to divert that attraction to a 'quadrennial meeting of the world" in which various venues of power may be created and retained. [In this way they have contributed to the winning-at-all-cost philosophy, the outrageous cheating, the arrant professionalism, and the miserly medal-counting.]

The crowds are inevitably thrilled by superlative athletic performances, but they are not allowed to savor them. Instead, their spontaneous cheers are organized for them and diverted to other considerations.

Their emotions are lifted—the appropriateness of that word is questionable unless a pickpocket analogy is applied—by matters quite irrelevant to the athletic performances.

Flags are marched out and raised and waved, anthems are played, great electronic fanfares are blared, and the medals are awarded by a pair of overaged worthies who have been made worthy to do so by contributing to these elaborate counter-athletic proceedings. [Ironically, spontaneous demonstrations of nationalistic feeling are prohibited by zealous security forces, as when some excited Finns attempted to join Lasse Viren, waving their blue and white banners, in his victory lap but were forcibly restrained from leaving the stands.]

So children throughout the stands, and perhaps throughout the world as they respond to the media coverage of the Games, cheer for countries often without being aware even of the names of the medal-winners.

And officials are aghast when American Mac Wilkens embraces East German Wolfgang Schmidt for his silver-medal discus throw, relegating American John Powell to the bronze. The idea that Wilkens, at this moment of his golden triumph, is a sportsman first and an American only incidentally is anathematic to the power structure. Never mind that it happens to be the truth.

The paramilitary aspect of the Olympics extends far beyond the awards ceremonies and the parades of competitors accompanied by the martial music. Judges and officials march out for every event. The attendants march in close-order drill to do everything—like carrying the baskets for runners to deposit their sweatsuits before their races. They even place and remove the hurdles in strict formation, getting off and on the carts in step.

It is ludicrous, unnatural, and absolutely unnecessary. It is as if bureaucratic man is insisting on imposing the arrogance of his orderliness upon the world. [All this business, however, is in polar opposition to man's nature and the nature of Olympic sport—the athlete performing to the best of his natural ability.

The antithesis between bureacratic man and natural man is clearly illustrated by an anecdote from the biography of Jack Higgs. He had completed his four-year tour of duty at the United States Naval Academy, and his parents had come up for the ceremonies from the little farming community out from Lewisburg, Tennessee, where the whole Higgs family had lived most of their lives. When the emotional barage of the final dress parade, the firing of the salute, and the surrendering of the guns was over, Jack met his folks at the statue of Tecumseh. Though he was all choked up, he managed to say, "Well, Daddy, what did you think of it?"

This wise and simple man answered, "Them birds sho did haul ass when they shot them guns."

Jack says that this response changed his whole life. He eventually renounced a military career, that most orderly model of bureaucratic man, and embraced a life of humanistic study and teaching wherein he can maintain some semblance of natural man. And both his active and his scholarly pursuit of sport have involved and paralleled his efforts to cut through the rigmarole of bureaucratic man to perceive the essence of natural man.

Let me present two examples from the Montreal Olympics of what is wrong with the proceedings, both from] the track and field competition, which to me is the core of the entire Games. No doubt there were many more, and perhaps these may seem trivial, but they occurred in full view of the fans in the stadium—and with those fans involved as object or subject of attention.

On Sunday, the women completed three events of the pentathlon, ending late in the afternoon with the high jump. Three competitors were left to try for 1.82 meters, Nadejda Tkachenko, Diane Jones, and Andrea Bruce. The three eventual medalists, Burglinde Pollak, Christine Laser, and Siegrun Siegl, already had gone out.

Bruce, who had yet to miss at any height, sailed gracefully over the bar on her first try. Jones and Tkachenko missed all three times. This made Bruce the winner, but since the pentathlon is decided on a point system [like the men's decathlon], it was important for the lithe Jamaican to go as high as she could to make up for her lack of strength in the shot put, in which she finished last.

She was preparing to make her first try at 1.84 meters—and the way she had been jumping, that looked like a cinch—when the pit was closed and all other activity stopped by the fanfare announcing a victory ceremony for an earlier event.

Then came the music, the announcements, the moments of glory for the portly awarder and his portlier accompanier, the waves to the crowds, the flags, the anthem, and the exit march.

During this six or seven minutes, I watched Andrea Bruce. She stood right where she had been, head down, trying to keep her concentration, trying to keep mind and body in that grooved state in which she had been jumping with such apparent ease.

When the patriotic theatrics were finally over, she jumped. She missed three times.

The ceremony had taken precedence over the event. [It was not even, as is the case with many sporting events, that the demands of television programming had altered the order of things to suit time slots and commercial impact. It was more like the kind of compulsive schedule-keeping that is often taken as the triumph of Il Duce's Italy: "At least Mussolini got the trains running on time." But it is more than symbolic; it is a purposeful ordering of priorities.]

If it is argued that the medalists deserve their moment of glory, it should be answered that such moments come in victory and are duly celebrated by victory laps and that the ceremonies themselves are anticlimactic to the athletes but fundamental to the nationalistic/militaristic structure of the athletics.

This point is clarified in the next example. Don Quarrie, Millard Hampton, and Dwayne Evans had blazed to the men's 200-meter medals. Hand-in-hand they were taking a victory lap, when the award ceremonies began for the 10,000 meters.

The athletes' natural celebration was preempted by the system's formalities, and part of the crowd booed—not, I'm afraid, because the victory lap was interrupted, but because these winners were not deferring to the orderly progression of those other celebrations, all that stuff that gives those fans their kicks. The bureaucracy has pushed those emotional highs on the crowds, and the crowds are hooked.

The remedy is to quit cold turkey. It's a drastic but simple solution. Leave all the flags and anthems home. The Olympics don't need "national" as a concept any more than they need "teams." If one country has the four best weightlifters in the world, what perverse application of the word "team" can dictate which one stays home?

Let the best compete against the best; for themselves and with the world. A model is provided by, of all things, the Indy 500. Let the competitors qualify, within a given period of time, for their event or events. It should not have to be on any given day—the absence of Steve Williams, Houston McTear, and Reggie Jones from the sprint events reminds us painfully of that.

It should have nothing to do with country, or size of delegation, or politics of selection (oh, yes, there's plenty of that everywhere), or politics of confrontation, or politics of any kind. How can there be a meeting of the world without a whole continent and the most populated country?

The people who control the Olympics can't let [such a pure sporting structure] happen. Their power is built on nationalistic national organizations, nurtured, by jingo, by working up patriotic fervor, and supported by the quick fix of paramilitary spectacle.

Take away the flags, and the flag-wavers will have nothing to hold on to. The Games will be for the athletes, and the sports fans will love them just as much, maybe more.

One side effect of this remedy, I'm afraid, as much as I love basketball especially, is the loss of team sports. Team sports adapt too readily to the chauvinistic ways of the present structure, and they will have to go.

It would be no great loss because most of the team sports have their own international competitions anyway, and the others could, too. Besides, in some cases the teams competing in the Olympics are nowhere near as good as the teams in international competition.

Let the purpose of the Games be the games, let the focus of attention be the action, and let those who participate in the action be the ones considered first in all policies.

And let the other people, with their titles and ribbons and flags and monies and bellies, have an oldtimers' day parade in the stadium early some morning. And let's see if anyone salutes.

When the sporting spirit in the Olympic Games themselves has been replaced by political, commercial, bureaucratic, expedient, and unethical considerations, there should be no surprise that similar corruption is found at every level of competition. But it is perhaps most shocking at the Little League level, where nothing like international prestige, national interests, and personal careers is at stake. It seems to me easier to swallow reports of attempted cheating by an Olympic fencer than to deal with the stories of attempted cheating in the Soapbox Derby, children conspiring with adults to win unfairly.

What is at stake in the Little League to make the competition so fierce as it has become? The rationale behind the organizations is admirable: give the young people a structure for their sports, opportunities for universal participation, proper equipment for their safety, and some adult leadership and coaching for their grasp of fundamentals and their improvement. But a kind of Gresham's Law of motivations takes over—the insidious drives out the altruistic. Reports of Little League activities are horror stories of the savaging of positive values.

Organizers of Little Leagues have taken positions of defending their organizations from dangerous outside influences—girls, blacks, Latinos, Taiwanese—thus coaching their players in such mature sporting attributes as exclusivity, xenophobia, chauvinism. In action, the kids suffer the manipulation of adults who are playing out fantasy roles of power in the image of professional sports, that is, in a microcosm of the Machiavellian scheming and the Lombardian driving they perceive as the keys to winning. The kids also suffer the consequences of commercialization even at the Little League level, where the best team (in terms of won-lost record) has the best chance of getting the best uniforms, outfitted by businesses that want their names on the jerseys of winners.

Perhaps worst of all, because the corruption is subtler, is the undermining of the positive values of team play in competition. This was succinctly expressed in part of a letter I received from a Wayne, Pennsylvania, mother after she heard one of my NPR interviews:

> I had just finished writing a letter to my son's hockey coach, asking that certain values be made explicit, both to the players and to their parents re: winning and losing, defense and offense, "stars" and supporters, equal playing time, "creaming" the opposition, and playing different positions.
>
> Competition *between* boys on the same team seemed to get out of hand recently. The leading scorer couldn't even congratulate my son when he made his first and only hat trick. Subsequently, the parental cheering from the stands during games was offensive to me.
>
> I think it would be better for the boys if their sports programs were better articulated with values I would like them to hold in the non-sporting world: pursuit of excellence, support for each other, team play, and respect for a developing skill.

Here was a woman with some apparent interest in sports to whom its devaluations were being brought home in forceful personal object lessons.

Most parents do not witness first-hand the color-war competitions in summer camps that I mentioned with favor in the last chapter, but they would probably approve. One of my students reported in her journal her own experience as counselor during color war, where she found "the most intense sense of competition I've ever seen exhibited by any age group, especially pre-teenagers." She worried about "the atmosphere surrounding the whole affair" and said,

> I know it affected me, and it must affect the kids who participate. I'd like to know what happens to those kids, how they turn out. Do they become terrifically successful because of the exposure to high-

powered competition and the obsessive need to win or does it crip-
ple them in some way? . . . We don't seem to be a people who play
games for fun and exercise, but we must elevate all competition to
heroic proportions.

I found these comments particularly appropriate since they
came from a person with her own extensive background in competitive sailing. She wrote about this in response to a remark Jack
Russell made in class about how involvement in sports can make
people learn how to lose.

I can't overemphasize how important this "learning how to lose"
is to the enjoyment of sport. And, unfortunately, most people never
really learn how to lose and therefore never really learn how to
enjoy winning.

My family has participated in small sailboat racing (15½ feet to 25
feet) since I was six years old. I was a popular crew on those light
wind days when every skipper is looking for a crew that weighs less
than 60 pounds. I guess osmosis went to work and I was sailing a
boat of my own (without knowing exactly what I was doing or why)
in Saltine races (young "salts").

It was a lot of fun at first. I just loved getting out in that boat, and
occasionally winning a trophy (a 59-cent candy bar or a large box of
popcorn) was great. I enjoyed winning them and losing just seemed
to be part of the game, sometimes. But when I got into the big time
and started racing in the regattas against my sisters and father and
mother, I got scared. Scared I would lose, scared I'd hit someone (I
did, once or twice), and scared that I wouldn't be as good as the
rest. And I wasn't as good.

But that wasn't the biggest problem. For several years I was so
afraid of losing that I had a hard time doing anything but. I would
castigate myself for every mistake. I would get so uptight and nervous that I couldn't think straight. Thinking back on that period all I
remember is losing a lot. Actually, I came in second often, but all I
could see was that I wasn't first.

I decided that the situation was driving me crazy, so I got out.

One summer I said, Dad, Mom, I'm not coming to the lake or to regattas this summer. I've got myself a job in Maine as a camp counselor teaching sailing and water skiing. After my summer away I did a lot of thinking and talking with friends about what I'd done to myself. I knew that I wanted to be able to enjoy winning and to do that I had to learn to lose. Until then no one had ever told me it was all right to come in second or third or whatever.

For the first time I truly realized that I could go out and sail that boat in a race for fun. Heresy, but I loved it. And I learned that I could sail in races when I wanted to, not because someone at the club thought I should. So the next spring I went back to the lake and tried my hand.

I went out to race and felt great. My father was sailing another boat, same class, and we started off right together. At the gun I was just a few inches ahead of him, but I didn't feel like throwing up. The wind felt great and the boat responded beautifully. We sailed a close race and I won. It felt good.

I didn't race all the time that summer, just occasionally when I felt like screaming into the wind because I was happy, or when I was so depressed that I needed to feel that adrenalin pumping through the veins. I won some, came in second or worse other times. The next summer, figuring it would be the last chance I'd have for a while, I decided to sail the entire season.

That year I was a big winner. Won the club championship, the class cup; finished second in the State and 14th, out of a field of 60, in the Nationals. I blew the district championship to hell and back; I had started to care just a little too much.

But it was a good summer. Before that I would never have considered a 14th out of anything worth mentioning, but I even felt good about that. Now sometimes I can get exhilarated just at the thought of being in that sailboat. Can you imagine anything that pleasurable making you sick? Well it doesn't do that to me anymore, or I don't do it to myself.

I have to remember where my values and priorities are. If I fall back into the old pattern I forget how good it feels to sail that boat. I don't want to lose that pleasure. Right now, in my mind's eye, I can see myself sailing on the lake. I can almost feel it—blue sky, big cumulus clouds, lots of wind, yes, I can feel it.

I have quoted at length from Patricia Farrell Mayo's journal for several reasons, but probably most of all because I wanted that reminder of the enormous pleasure of competitive sport when the sport maintains its ascendancy over the result, when the structure serves the content not itself. If there were not such great value in the sports, they would not be worth saving from the corruption and subversion. But I suppose if the sports were not such potent forces in our lives, they wouldn't be worth the efforts of those who would coopt, corrupt, and subvert them.

Theoretically a system of ethics based on sport would be as idealistic as a Grantland Rice poem or a peroration from Jack Armstrong to Billy and Betty. It would rely on the values of things in themselves, on intrinsic worth, on the pursuit of excellence for its own sake, and on a healthy balance of self- and group-satisfactions. But in contemporary practice, sports teach an ethic of ulterior motives, of ends justifying means, of putting numbers (often along with dollar signs) on everything. It is Conn Smythe saying that if we don't find a way of stopping the violence in hockey we're going to have to print more tickets.

At every level of competition, athletes, who could find in sports ways of controlling aggressive, destructive behavior, are instead instructed that no violence in the cause of victory is too extreme and that, when success is measured in income, violence may be rewarding even without victory. Instead of the sport providing a structure for the improvement of the breed of athletes and the edification of the public at large, we have society cheapening (and quantifying) the values of sport and sports destroying the values of the athletes.

During the PGA championship at Congressional, I walked a few holes during the second round with Tommy Watson's wife. Watson, a bright, articulate, boyishly charming Stanford graduate, might not seem to be typical of the touring golf professional or the PGA establishment. Indeed, as Linda Watson, herself a Mills graduate, said, he is probably the only guy on the tour who was a McGovernite in 1972. But he's changed, she said. "Our earnings on the tour put us in a tax bracket where we have to be concerned with protecting what we have." Still, Tommy Watson is concerned with using his position to make a contribution. He and his close friend Buddy Allin sponsored a benefit which realized $16,000. The recipient was a fund for golf scholarships at Stanford. I wondered what the ex-McGovernite view was with respect to the question of why there should *be* golf scholarships at Stanford, but I didn't ask. The values of the Watsons are no more and no less than what the PGA might say they should be. There are no different drummers beating paths over the golf courses. The players, like the galleries, are told where and how to walk, what and when to speak.

Because of the great disparity between the ideal values of sports in theory and the expedient values that obtain in practice, the public is spoon-fed cant and hypocrisy by the cracker barrel. Philosophers of sport appear under every byline and press release, and the phenomenon of the coach as shaman is an affront to our awareness that would be ludicrous if the men in the long-billed caps weren't taken so seriously.

A pit stop on the New Jersey Turnpike is named for Vince Lombardi, who thus takes his place with Walt Whitman, Thomas Edison, Joyce Kilmer, Clara Barton, and Molly Pitcher as an authenticated culture hero. Lombardi's blend of relentless toughness and gruff sentimentality was what passed for integrity in the sporting world, but he is best known for the motto that a world of cynical sports fans has embraced as the alpha and omega. Whether he said, "Winning isn't the most important thing, wanting to win is," as Robert Riger says, or "Winning isn't the most important thing, it's the only thing," the philosophy is aptly summed up therein. The motto has been taken as a justification for methods Lombardi would never have approved, but that seems almost irrelevant in the face of wholesale acceptance of the mythos that goes with the logos. Similarly, an offhand quip by a verbally prodigal baseball manager, Leo Durocher, has become veritable gospel: "Nice guys finish last." Even the utterances of such vernacular-manglers as Casey Stengel, Yogi Berra, and Wes Westrum have come into our lore as the obiter dicta of venerable elders, so that when a commentator like Jack Whitaker suggests that for all of him Pete Rose should get the Nobel Prize for his attitude toward and style of playing baseball it only seems *relatively* absurd.

Several of our bigtime college football coaches are thought of as eminent sages. It is still a matter of wonderment that Bud Wilkinson was not able to step smartly from the Sooners to the Senate. The guess here is that Woody Hayes and Bear Bryant would find the going much smoother now in Ohio and Alabama. George F. Will once wrote that "In Alabama George Wallace can be elected governor only because The Bear, molder of men for the Crimson Tide, cannot be bothered with lesser offices." A political columnist, Will often devotes his space to sports-related topics. One of his most memorable pieces was called "The Wrath of Woody Hayes," which included the following gems:

> Hayes thinks [football] is Kulturkampf pitting the religion of sacrifice against the slothfulness of our lax age.
>
> . . . crusade for the stern virtues of pain and discipline that Hayes says produce winning football team and civilizations.
>
> . . . things (like good losers and people who take vacations) that the modern world would be better off without.
>
> civilization is built by winners, people who scorn delights, live exhausting days and keep the ball on the ground.
>
> He favors the running game because it favors those who can administer and absorb pain, two abilities that mark life's winners. "If it comes easy," Hayes says, "it isn't worth a damn." He thinks the forward pass is a modernist heresy, worse than gun control and almost as bad as deficit spending.

The tone of the piece is sardonic, but Will's wit doesn't completely cover the admiration that the philosphical conservative has for the football coach:

Hayes, like bouillabaisse, is an acquired taste. But in an age of plastic politicians, and professors professing the day's flaccid consensus, and tradesmen who can't do their jobs, Hayes is a glorious anachronism.

Will's final point is a psycho-sociological observation that suggests a currency to the anachronism. He supposes widespread popular support from Hayes, "legions, nationwide, the closet Woody freaks [who] are not quite sure what he is, but . . . know he is no imitation."

I'd like to think that Will is wrong, that whatever is "glorious" about Hayes—the twin colossi of his anger and his ego—does not have mass appeal; but I fear that he is right. Those reporters who have been slugged or threatened by him for asking the wrong questions, the photographers and players who have been kicked by him for blocking his way or thwarting his will, they are minority voices, small squeals in a wilderness of values. As long as Woody goes on winning, his violent actions will be taken as winsome and his pompous blather as wisdom.

Look at what unprecedented winning has done to the retired basketball coach at UCLA. He has become even more than the "Wizard of Westwood," he has become an elder statesman, a sage, a fount of inspiration. John Wooden has proved himself to be one of the greatest basketball coaches of all, just as he was one of the greatest players, but what has qualified him to preach morality to the multitudes? He has constructed a "Pyramid of Success," duly copyrighted, which he takes as the text for his sermons, and it might be taken merely as a monument to presumptuousness were it not for other factors including his position of influence as a sports legend.

George Will likened Woody Hayes to a figure of American Gothic out of a Grant Wood painting, but Jim Murray had long since made the same observation about Wooden—and with greater appropriateness. Wooden's pyramid is made up of qualities, fifteen in blocks and ten more along the sides, which are defined in platitudes (e.g., ENTHUSIASM—"Your heart must be in your work") or not at all (e.g., INTEGRITY—"speaks for itself"), leading to the summit. There, success is defined as "peace of mind which is a direct result of self-satisfaction in knowing you did your best to become the best that you are capable of becoming."

If there were building codes for such structures, Wooden's pyramid would never pass the tests for logic, concreteness, consistency, or coherence. But it is the test for applicability that I would administer here. The fact is that John Wooden achieved his own considerable success not through FRIENDSHIP, LOYALTY, SELF-CONTROL, ADAPTIBILITY, PATIENCE, and FAITH "Through prayer" (to take some of his key terms), but because of his fierce, aggressive competitiveness, his unswerving determination to reach his goals, his total devotion to the rightness of his own ways, and his impatient striving for higher levels of competence. The pyramid is worse than a monument to bad taste; it is an icon of pious hypocrisy. Is this what success in sports means—that you do whatever you have to do to win, so that when you do you can make any pretense of virtue you want? Apparently, Americans are willing to accept anything at all from a winner, and the bigger the winner the more shit we can swallow from him.

To do justice to this subject, the reverence devoted to coaches as wise men, one would have to devote a volume, a large one, perhaps called *The Wit and Wisdom of Our National Leaders (or What Passes for Same in a Jockocracy)*. I will limit myself to one more egregious example, but it will come in the next chapter where the subject matter calls for it.

What coaches and other influential leaders of the sports establishment do not understand is that the conservative tendency of sports structures not to change, their unwillingness even to adapt to changing external conditions, may be self-destructive. If, instead of reading only the box scores and the orthodox gospels according to Lombardi, Durocher, and Napoleon, they read some of the heretical texts by such disparate writers as Jack Scott, Harry Edwards, and George Leonard, they might perceive some of the dangers they court.

Even better, they might read Robert Coover's brilliant second novel, *The Universal Baseball Association, J. Henry Waugh, Prop*. It is the story of a man who has invented a three-dice baseball game and then created a world around it. He not only keeps complete statistics for the twenty-one "men" on each of the eight squads but also conceives personalities for them all along with managers, writers, old-timers, fans, etc. The mythology of baseball yields songs and ballads, as well as legends, and gradually Waugh withdraws more and more from his "real" life as an accountant to live through the lives of his creations in his created world.

Waugh's emotional involvement with his invention leads to a number of problems, mostly concerned with rules. On one level, the rules of his own life are broken. He knows that "over the long haul he needed that balance, that rhythmic shift from house to house, and he knew that total one-sided participation in the league would soon grow even more oppressive than his job at Dunkelmann, Zauber and Zifferblatt." Yet he does become obsessed with the league and loses both his balance (an accountant's most grievous loss) and his job. On another level, he is led to override the rules of the game itself, altering the chance dictation of the dice because he is determined to achieve certain results for particular players. The game comes to be more and more lifelike, and Waugh rationalizes that "the circuit wasn't closed, his or any other: there were patterns, but they were shifting and ambiguous and you had a lot of room inside them."

This issue, in turn, leads to parallel considerations within the UBA. There, Chancellor Fenn McCaffree muses, "What if . . . we have passed, without knowing it, from a situation of sequential compounding into one of basic and finite yes-or-no survival, causing a shift of what you might call the equilibrium point, such that the old strategies, like winning ball games, sensible and proper within the old stochastic or recursive sets, are, under the new circumstances, *insane!*" In the next-to-last chapter, McCaffree's suspicions gain some credibility in "an ancient yet transformed ritual." The final chapter is a dazzling literary display in which all the novel's threads and themes are brought together and then projected forward in a new configuration. Waugh has been completely submerged in his created world, and that world has changed in ways that seem beyond anyone's control.

If some of Coover's novelistic philosophy could crack through the rock-ribbed attitudes of the sporting establishment, the lesson of healthy adaptability over insane intransigence might fortify their positions. But there is a corollary lesson to be found in such films as *Roller Ball, Death Race 2,000* and *They Shoot Horses, Don't They?* It is the lesson of the destructive capacity of radical change. These are stories in which rules of competition are whimsically shifted without regard to the competitors. These opposite patterns have one thing in common: the values of the games themselves are subordinated to others, either the self-interest of management or another irrelevancy.

At a second remove from sport is the all-too-common superimposition of the profit motive. Ironically this intrinsic element of the American way is destructive of the structure of competition that is itself emblematic of the American way. But of all the agents that wither the garlands in the crown of sports, the most insidious is the closest to home. Winning the game becomes more important than the game, and this transvaluation seems especially deeply ingrained in the American psyche, as George Plimpton among many others has said.

It was not so very long ago that a genuine cultural revolution seemed to be taking place in our country, in Charles Reich's best-selling phrase a "greening of America." There was to be a growing acceptance of the values and priorities of the younger generation: peace rather than aggressiveness, respect rather than assertiveness, doing your own thing rather than repressiveness, tolerance rather than paternalism, conservation rather than gross national product, environmental protection rather than ecologically destructive growth, commonality rather than exclusivity, sharing rather than owning, and playing rather than winning. "Make love not war," said the bumper stickers and T-shirts, in summary of what it was all supposed to be about.

How have we passed so quickly into a phase I call the "graying of the greening"? The common denominator in all the qualities, concepts, and institutions condemned by the counterculture is competitiveness. Competition structures more than our athletic activities, more than our political, economic, legal, and educational lives, more than our artistic striving for prizes and grants and recognition. Competition is at the heart of our social interacting. We still win the hands of spouses and the intimacy of friends, and seductions are scores, so that even making love instead of war is just a rechanneling of the competitive drive. The rewards of life are won; punishments are the price of losing, being beaten.

The conditioning is massive and so deeply entrenched that the revolution could never turn it over. The idea of not winning was generally if illiberally translated into losing. Playing, that is, living, without caring about winning, that is, achieving in terms that can be measured, simply makes no sense; in our culture, that mode of thought does not compute. From Archie Bunkerdom through the heartland to the place where Lucy dwells (from low C to shiny see?), the counterculture was called a bunch of losers. With more bravado than vision, the visionaries said, all right, it's all right to lose, let's be proud of being nonwinners.

At such a turning point in consciousness, the whole cause was lost. Because causes, too, are won, like the hearts and minds of people. Societies are won over to new ways of thinking when they seem to be better. Revolutions are successful when they win out over established ways in competitive struggles. The refusal to compete is an acknowledgment of defeat. The movement became inertia.

There remain a few isolated cases of people who espouse alternate ways and live by them. But they are the cellar-dwellers of our civilization-league, souls lost in a space of alienation, outside the centripetal forces of competition in our culture. And I suppose that is appropriate for losers.

# VI

# ACTION AND THE PURITAN ETHIC

Talk about confusion of values. Our society has promulgated the unique notion that while sports of all kinds are good, gambling on sports is bad. Never mind that the two are universally inseparable, that some form of stakes is always a part of the game and in many cases defines the game. "It is axiomatic," as has been said in an analysis of the basketball scandals, "that wherever games are played there will be action, and it is no semantic accident that action is a synonym for gambling."

The present situation is confusing, anomalous, and hypocritical, but some understanding of how it developed can come from a sketchy bit of cultural history. To begin, consider the traditional beauty contest, viewed by many American audiences as another form of athletic competition. Pick the winners of each event, pick the semifinalists, and pick Miss Whateveritis. The stakes are relatively large, but betting is not customary—at least not now.

The beauty pageant is not an American invention, however. One early competition in ancient Greece had the Torjan prince Paris in the role of Bert Parks awarding the prize to Aphrodite. This story is a curious one, with built-in ironies of its own. But it is especially instructive for this investigation when seen in a larger context. There, it is an integral part of a whole series of related stories.

Basically the story is simple and straightforward. Eris, the goddess of discord (later to be embodied in the magic mirror on the wall of Snow White's wicked stepmother), had thrown down a golden apple inscribed "For the Fairest" in a company including Hera, Athena, and Aphrodite. Zeus, in his infinite wisdom, refused to pass judgment, that is, to choose among sister-wife and daughters (or nieces, depending on which genealogy one accepts). Instead he sent Hermes to Mount Ida where Paris herded cattle, ordering the handsome young mortal to arbitrate.

Paris, making the best of a difficult situation, accepted the charge and asked to see each goddess naked one at a time—the ancient version of the swimsuit competition apparently would be decisive. Hera came down the runway first, offering Paris all of Asia and the greatest wealth in the world if he picked her. Paris examined her appreciatively but rejected the bribe. Next came Athena, offering to make the judge victorious in all battles and the wisest, handsomest man in the world. Again Paris dealt reasonably with the bribe offer.

Aphrodite was less direct, except that she came close enough to him to embarrass Paris. She talked about Helen, describing her as equal in beauty and passion to herself, arousing Paris first and only then promising him Helen's love. Winner hands down in woman's wiles as well as beauty, Aphrodite thus got the golden apple award from Paris and won the destruction of Troy from the vengeful Hera and Athena.

Paris was only mortal, after all. In a sense Aphrodite had offered him herself, love, embodied in her human mirror-image, Helen. In the traditional folktale format, the hero is offered a choice of caskets or doors—a choice of wealth, wisdom, or love (the three forms of power)—and his decision has a significance that goes far beyond his own fate. What significance do we find in this particular version? It is a beauty competition, and the most beautiful contestant has won. All have used unfair methods, but only the subtlest cheater has benefited. Yet the winner of the title deserves, by her very nature, to have won. Is virtue its own reward, or does victory go to the one who successfully disguises the bending of rules? Both clearly, but neither. What has the winner won? The distinction inherent in the championship? No—she already owned the distinction. She has won the stake—the golden ball with the words on it—and the losers go off empty-handed.

Aphrodite's spoils as victor are apparently meager. Paris's spoils come to include not only Helen but the treasures they carry off from Sparta and Sidon on the way to Troy. Ultimately it is the Greeks who despoil Troy. The preliminary question remains of why Paris is Zeus's choice of beauty-contest judge, and in the answer to that lies a clue to the whole context of contests and prizes.

Paris, a prince of Troy but abandoned as an infant on Mount Ida for oracular reasons that need not concern us here, grew to be beautiful, intelligent, and strong, as befitted his noble birth. While herding cattle, he amused himself by staging bullfights (bull against bull) and crowning the winner with flowers, the losers with straw. When he had determined on a champion bull he pitted it against the best of other herds and beat all challengers. He then offered a golden crown for any bull that could beat his. Ares turned himself into a bull to get some of that action and Paris paid off without hesitation. This fair-dealing openhandedness in judging a competition was what pleased the gods and earned Paris his reputation.

That reputation was considerably enhanced a short time later. Priam, it seems, presided over annual games to memorialize his son's death, with a bull from Paris's herd as one prize. When his own champion bull was chosen one year, Paris himself went off to Troy. He won the crown for boxing and two crowns for foot-racing, before the embarrassed and jealous princes tried to kill him. At this point his identity was revealed and the family reconciled. Paris not only attended his own funeral but won the most prizes and his rightful place and fame and fortune too. The conflagration that finally resulted cannot detract from Paris's triumphant return and performance.

One more story, parallel in some particulars, is appropriate here, the story of Atalanta. Like Paris, this royal child was abandoned in infancy and suckled by a she-bear. And like Paris she grew to be a champion, as hunter and runner, drawing first blood in hunting the Calydonian Boar and defeating all challengers in foot-races. The stakes for her races were heavy. When she won, the defeated suitor would be killed and she retained her sacred virginity; if she lost, the winner would win her hand and land in marriage.

The issue was complicated by the suit of Melanion, assisted by Aphrodite, who had considerable experience in influencing the result of contests. She gave Melanion three golden apples, ordinarily the prize for victory. In the race, he distracts Atalanta by throwing the apples, and by stopping to pick them up, Atalanta in effect throws the race. It is the earliest recorded fixed race. Melanion wins the race and Atalanta, Atalanta gets the golden apples and loses her virginity, and the wages of the sins of both—unfair handicap, failure to concentrate on the race—is death, or at least metamorphosis.

The point of this series of stories lies in their common denominator—competition for a prize, whether or not in purely athletic contests. But the idea of stakes is hardly limited to ancient Hellenic material. The Greeks may have been explicit about their gods' insistence on fair play and fair earning of prizes fairly awarded, but the fact is that such ideas are universally found among ancient material of every tradition. Games and sports of every primitive and sophisticated kind are inseparable from the stakes involved.

This does not mean that the competition is played for the sake of the prize; it only means that the prize structures the competition. The game or sport does not serve the stake; it is the stake that serves the sport or game. Taken as universal mythic analogues, these stories all say that death or mortality structures life. But it would be a perversion to suppose that life is lived in the service of death. Indeed, radical forms of sacrilege often assert this perverse supposition. What is significant for the present argument is that life is meaningless outside a context that includes death, just as the idea of competition is meaningless outside a context that includes a prize to be won.

From a variety of ancient traditions come vestiges of high-stakes competition, including the riddling games universally familiar in mythology, the common practice of athletic games to honor gods at festivals, and the presence of such figures as the seven Japanese gods of luck. I limit myself to five specific examples here: (1) from Central America, where there was a ball court at every temple, a myth tells of Quetzalcoatl's contest with Tlaloc, the rain god, and winning a choice of prizes—either practical maize or symbolic jade and fine feathers; (2) from Egypt, where the stories of conflict between Horus and Set include a marathon swimming contest with the throne of the gods at stake; (3) from Polynesia, where there are many tales about *kupua* or tricksters who compete with gods in both riddling games and feats of strength, usually to acquire some gift for mankind; (4) from Scandinavia, where the Old Norse Edda tells how the giant Hrungnir beat Odin in a horse race, drank from Thor's goblets (reminiscent of the champagne for Grand Prix winners after a victory lap), but lost a duel to Thor, who thus preserved Asgard; and (5) from India, where the epic *Mahabharata* tells of the tournament held to celebrate the completion of the Pandavas' formal education.

In this final example, the tournament gives way to single combat in which Arjuna kills Karna. Later, too, there is an archery contest to see who will win the hand of Draupadi. (Currently, Emmylou Harris sings of how the jesters flock around her, vying to win her favors, "to see which one will take the Queen of the Silver Dollar home.") The single combat of champions is the clearest case in point here. From our own Old Testament traditions we have parallel cases like David versus Goliath in battle or Elijah versus the Philistine priests in efficient prayer/ritual where their respective nations have staked their freedom and future on the result of the event. In other words, the spectators are heavily involved in the stakes of the contest.

In the development of our civilization's attitudes, a significant change took place in Catholic medieval Europe. The Church, led in part by superstitious taboos associated with the Crucifixion, in part by a scholastic compulsion to flesh out a symmetrical concept of deadly sins, and in part by a genuine human concern for the damage in all forms of excessive pleasure, legislated the vice of gambling up into a type of the sin of Sloth. All four Gospels include the detail of Roman soldiers gambling for Christ's raiment, but the significance of the detail was lost upon the moralizers. There should have been no opprobrium attached to the gambling, only an ironic horror that Jesus's things were treated just like everyone else's, since the gambling itself was universally regarded at the time as a fair and equitable means for the redistribution of booty.

As far as the seven deadly sins were concerned, the popular view was quite different from the scholastic. The best chart of medieval thinking is supplied by Dante in his *Commedia*. There is not a mention of gambling in any of the circles of the damned in the *Inferno*. When Ciacco the glutton raises his head in the third circle, one looks in vain for a slothful companion. In the fourth circle, the avaricious hoarders are matched with profligate wasters, but neither gambling nor sloth is associated with the waves of torment here.

In fourteenth-century England we look to Gower, Langland, and Chaucer for the full range of commonly accepted opinion. The "moral Gower" classified seven types of sloth (*accidie*) in his *Confessio Amantis:* Lachesce (procrastination), Pusillamite (lack of heart to undertake the duty of a man), Foryetelnesse (forgetfulness), Negligence, Idleness, Somnolence, and Tristesse (despondency). Only in the depiction of the fifth type is there a hint that gamblers have a place among the slothful: Idleness is an evil character who is idle in all seasons and all places, *unless he's shooting craps ("bot if he pleie oght ate Dees")*. But Idleness only does anything or uses any winnings to get into a situation where he won't have to do anything else. The sidewise slap at gambling is gratuitous, and only this particular gambler and the sinful waste of winnings are condemned.

In *Piers the Ploughman*, Langland presents a quick allegorical cavalcade of the seven deadlies. Sloth comes last, after Glutton, but there's not a trace of the gambler about him. Later, when Piers is setting the world to work, he promises sufficient food for all, but excepts Jack the juggler, Janet from the stews, Daniel the dice-player, Doll the whore, Friar Rogue and his Order, and Robin the ribald with his bawdy jokes. The common denominator is making a false living, but these are characters, after all, who do not need a welfare state. The puritanical elements of Langland's attitude will get fuller attention shortly.

In his *Canterbury Tales*, Chaucer takes a broad view of gambling but not necessarily a dim one. The tales themselves, for example, get underway by lot as the Knight pulls the short straw in what may be a fixed drawing. In the fragmentary "Cook's Tale," the hero is Perkyn Revelour, an apprentice who is a champion at having fun. Among his several talents he can throw dice as well as anyone in town, and he is as generous with his winnings as he is generous with his master's goods when he is losing. Perkyn's fate remains unknown as the tale stops well short of the Cook's intention or his moral, and we have no benefit of commentary from anyone on the Canterbury pilgrimage about the gambling reveler.

In "The Pardoner's Tale," the arch-hypocrite tells a story of revelers, too, in the form of a sample sermon. The Pardoner's text is *radix malorum est cupiditas*, but the tale involves all of the seven deadly sins. Here again gambling (specifically *hasard*, the Middle English version of craps) is associated with drunkenness, gluttony, and lechery in these debauched rioters, but any condemnation is a matter of guilt by association—over half a millennium before Senator Joseph McCarthy's time. Chaucer's references elsewhere, in the Man of Law's Prologue and *Troilus and Criseyde*, show both his familiarity with the game of *hasard* and its acceptance as a common frame of reference.

To the medieval Catholic, the realities of everyday experience, which included gambling as a natural matter of course, were not condemned simply because an ideal, moral concept was fervently cherished on a spiritual level. But there were reformers; there was a puritanical streak, not only in a Langland but even in a Chaucer. Chaucer's Parson, who is accused of being a Lollard or Wycliffite, has the honor of telling the final tale, and it is a straightforward sermon on sin and penitence. Once more the treatment of Sloth fails to include any mention of gambling, but the Parson throughout emphasizes the two elements that lead in time to the second phase of revaluation concerning gambling: the praise of hard work and the condemnation of anything that is fun.

What Michael Novak calls "the severe Puritan bias of America" now takes over and dominates the revaluation. Where gambling had been elevated to sinhood, it is now legislated into a crime. Alone of the descendants of Western Christian civilization, the United States has taken the puritanical attitudes toward gambling and made them official. Thus the multiple hypocrisies of the contemporary situation. Where medieval European society was comfortable with the conflicting worldly and moralistic views side by side, twentieth-century America has adopted the uncomfortabe posture of burying its head in the sand.

The federal government presumably follows the Tenth Amendment in leaving to the States all decisions regarding gambling. Yet the Immigration and Naturalization Service will deny citizenship to anyone who has "received income mostly from illegal gambling." Such behavior is taken as proof of bad moral character, just like polygamy, adultery, prostitution, illegal entry, habitual drunkenness, and trafficking in drugs. These are the seven deadly sins as codified by the INS.

Opposition to gambling on moral grounds in the United States is often voiced, but only by those who refuse to examine the assumptions of their position. The potential for excess, abuse, and self-destruction is no doubt present in gambling—as it is in virtually every aspect of living—but that is not grounds for moralistic proscription. By that reasoning, all systems of government and law would be condemned because they are potentially corruptible, all eating would be evil because gluttony exists, all breathing bad because some air is polluted.

Yet despite the official moral judgment accepted in this society, some form of legalized gambling is officially condoned in thirty-three states. If sports are a big business, legalized gambling is a far bigger one, and illegal gambling is a gigantic conglomerate. Andrew Beyer has said, "Once we get over the hurdle, the notion that it's somehow immoral, that American athletes will be somehow contaminated, legalized sports betting will be universal." Yet on an individual level, there appears to be no moralistic hurdle at all, since most adults gamble and those who patronize illegal gambling operations do so without laying prohibitive odds on their consciences. The official public morality of the nation, then, is clearly at odds with the private, individual morality of most of its citizens, so that we must look for the operative, practical reasons for antigambling laws.

The Commission on the Review of the National Policy toward Gambling commissioned the Survey Research Center of the University of Michigan to chart betting behavior and attitudes in this country. One result of the sampling corroborated other published figures of over $17 billion gambled legally in 1974. Almost half of that amount was wagered in parimutuel betting at thoroughbred, standardbred, quarterhorse, and greyhound race tracks and jai alai frontons. And the lion's share of that figure was the total handle at the horse tracks. "Horse-racing," says Andrew Beyer, author of *Picking Winners* and a columnist on racing and gambling for the *Washington Star,* "is probably more of a culture than a sport. More than other sports it generates a sub-culture around it." The lives of many people in this special world, whether on the backstretch or in the clubhouse, revolve around gambling, and the fact that it is legal or the question of whether it is moral seems to mean nothing.

Beyer has talked of this world in other terms: "the intellectual stimulation of sitting down with a racing form and doping out a race beats other challenges; there's no ambiguity; you have the immediate satisfaction of knowing whether you're right or wrong; and if you're right you have the greater satisfaction of knowing that you've done something that few others can do." Clearly there are moral judgments implicit in such a point of view, but they stand outside the official moralizing by the arithmetical purity of their ethical definitions. A Beyerian horse-player wants to be at the track to make his bets for many practical reasons, but if he can't be there he wants to place his bet with whoever will take it. And there is always someone to take it, the nature of human systems of private enterprise being to provide for all social needs somehow or other whenever there is willingness to pay.

In the face of an official antigambling morality, thirty-three states and hundreds of smaller jurisdictions within them take the position that since they cannot legislate the evil out of existence they can at once benefit from it and control it. The benefits are entirely financial—an additional source of revenue—and they have been less than anticipated in most cases. The controls have been unsatisfactory, too. Because of the stress on revenue, legalized gambling takes such a heavy slice out of the handle that little if any inroads have been made into the volume of illegal betting. Though the policing of legal gambling is often less than adequate, there is at least the factor of public scrutiny to provide a measure of pressure on the maintenance of integrity.

The same survey that accurately approximated the volume of legal gambling was absurdly mistaken in its estimate of illegal gambling. The Michigan academicians put it at a little over 5 billion for 1974. The Justice Department's estimate was 29 to 39 billion. John Scarne, whose word on gambling is not to be taken lightly, makes it 500 billion. Could the scholarly research have been off by 99 percent? It seems outrageous to say so, and yet an examination of its figures and its methods shows great gaps of information, intelligence, and understanding. The Justice Department's estimate, by the way, is based on wiretap evidence and would tend to be low because of the limitations on their sources of information. But this is guesswork. It is better to proceed on the basis of the survey's own figures.

A little less than half of the estimated illegal gambling was assigned to "sports books," that is, betting on sporting events with bookmakers. It is this figure of $2,341,000,000 I am concerned with here. The survey was conducted with traditional methods of gathering samplings of public opinion, using a proven formula of establishing a demographically meaningful cross-section. But even granting the accuracy of method, two overwhelming errors appear: (1) the fear or suspicions of those polled regarding revelations of personal gambling data; (2) the ignorance of those polled (multiplied by that of the pollsters) concerning the volume of their own action. In other words, small or occasional gamblers or nongamblers would have reliable, relatively accurate figures, while active gamblers would not or could not supply anything resembling accurate totals.

I remember meeting at the track one day a gambler who had been polled. "Hey, Doc," he said, "I was a sampled gambler yesterday."

"What did you tell them, Louie?"

"The truth. They promised it was confidential."

"What did they ask?"

"They wanted to know an average football week end. I give 'em last week. I make eight hundred on Dallas lose five on Oakland."

"Did you tell them three hundred net?"

"No, thirteen hundred."

"Wait a minute. At 11–10 you laid 1430."

"Well I didn't count the vigorish."

"And you didn't count the other half-dozen games you bet."

"I broke even on those."

"But that's almost another thousand in the handle. You forget that? And the three or four $25 parleys you tried? And the Monday night game, with an if and reverse with two or three other games and the half dozen college games? Louie, you told them thirteen hundred and your average week is about four thousand."

"Well, it's all on paper, anyway."

Louie is not a big bettor, but because he tends to break even or close to it on his sports gambling he miniaturizes his total handle in a fraction of perhaps ¼, perhaps ⅛. Yet relative to the average size of the handle reported by the survey, he is a veritable Bet a Million Gates or Diamond Jim. If he is fairly representative (and in many important ways he is), the commission's $2.3 billion becomes, conservatively, 12 billion.

Now most of this money goes to the neighborhood corner entrepreneur. And most of *his* action is one-sided. In an average metropolitan area of say 300,000 souls, there may be twenty-odd bookmakers who are *not* gamblers. When they get unbalanced books on games of local interest or televised games (most of their action is in these categories), they have to lay it off or risk extinction. Each community of this size will have at least one bookies' bookie to handle this imbalance, which is in the 40 to 50 percent range of the neighborhood man's handle. The bigger man, in turn, will be forced to lay off 25 to 30 percent of his action at a central clearing house, usually within the state. And where large imbalances show up here, even the biggies must venture into the dangerous area of interstate commerce to lay off 10 to 15 percent. The original $12 billion bet by the gamblers has now become a $20-billion handle simply because the bookies don't want to gamble.

And so far, we're only talking about the small-timers, from the Louies on down. The real action goes directly to the second level (bookies' bookie) or higher by the big gambler. These are the high rollers who are never reached by the pollsters, and they make up the overwhelming bulk of the handle. Estimates range up to 80 percent, but if we say just 60 percent, then the $20 billion becomes $50 billion when the layoffs are factored in. I make it 6–5 that the commission's figure of $2.341 billion is no more than 3 (three) percent of the money bet on sporting events in this country in a calendar year.

The commission's recommendations, based in part on the misconceptions fostered by the Michigan people's survey, stand firmly on the Tenth Amendment. Let the states decide. Status quo. There was also, however, the recommendation to exempt wagers from federal excise taxes and to exempt gambling winnings (from legal operations) from federal income taxes. At least this acknowledges the realities of the federal government's incursions upon the state's sovereignty in gambling matters. But in disregard for the essential realities that obtain for the present discussion, the commission opposed legalization of sports-by-event gambling until there are basic changes in existing federal tax policies.

As a result of the Crime Control Acts of 1968 and 1970, according to a bookmaker who is one of the most honorable men of my acquaintance, "the United States government (under heavy disguise) has the right to come into a state and enforce that state's gambling laws." Essentially a political conservative, he has become incensed over the hypocritical invasions of privacy under specious moralistic pretenses. "If Congress (therefore the government and the people) doesn't want gambling to exist, then let's amend the Constitution and outlaw it completely. But if Congress doesn't want to do that, then let the individual states handle the gambling problem as the Supreme Court says they should and make the FBI quit trying to enforce state laws under the guise that gambling affects interstate commerce."

In a vain attempt to tap into the massive flow of gambling monies, the government has imposed an excise ("wagering") tax of 10 percent (since changed to 2 percent) on the gross. The revenue thus achieved is negligible. The effects have been to drive bookies further underground or turn them into gamblers themselves. Again I cite the independent entrepreneur:

> there are very few "bookies" left, those who have two-way action on every game to have the vigorish going for them. Before the interstate gambling laws were passed, a lot of "bookies" got two-way action on almost every game and, indeed, were assured of a profit. But now most "bookies" are isolated into their own small area and have only one-way action on most games, so they are not "bookies"

in the real sense of the word but rather they are actually gamblers just as the bettor is gambling when he places a bet. The vigorish does come into play, but not as practically everyone thinks it does. For example: if I have eleven hundred dollars on Tennessee and the same amount on Alabama, then barring a tie, I am assured of one hundred dollars profit. But if I pay the government ten percent of my gross, which in the above example would be ten percent of $2,200.00 or $220.00, then I will be loser $120.00 regardless of the outcome; and if the game ended in a tie, I suppose technically, I would owe the government $220.00 and, therefore, would be $220.00 loser.

Assuming that a "bookie" is paying his ten percent wagering taxes, he cannot actually "book" and stay in business. He is forced to gamble, not only because he gets one-way action, but because he must win enough on each game to pay the ten percent tax and still make a profit. If he accepts $1,800.00 on Tennessee and accepts $600.00 on Alabama, he has to pray that Alabama wins. If he has twenty such games, such as the one above, then if he can win a majority, or even less of them, he quits winner for the day, even after paying Uncle Sam. If he loses just four such games he will quit loser for the day; but if he loses six or seven, or more, he has had a disastrous day! Even if he is cheating on Uncle Sam by not paying wagering taxes, he is still clobbered. However, I think most "bookies" will have six or seven such disproportionate games, and the other thirteen or fourteen will be within two or three hundred dollars of being balanced which thereby reduces his chance of being clobbered in any one day.

The above is why I say there are few "bookies," but lots of "gamblers."

All this brings up the question of why Congress passed such a wagering tax in the first place. Did Congress want to eliminate gambling (or rather "bookies") by such law? If they did, then they only succeeded in driving the "bookies" underground, because they can't pay the 10 percent wagering tax and, therefore, can't pay any income tax if they happen to make a profit for the year.

If Congress wanted additional revenue, then why didn't they make the tax about one half of 1 percent, thereby permitting the "bookie" an opportunity to make a profit, pay his wagering tax, and also pay income tax.

I simply think Congress has never had the guts to outlaw gambling altogether, or to legalize it, but would rather use discriminatory tactics, such as the 10-percent wagering tax, trying to rid the country of "bookies." They know there is no way a person can "book" bets and pay 10 percent of his gross. It is simply mathematically impossible!

Of all the witnesses who paraded before the House Select Committee on Professional Sports in 1976, not one favored the legalization of gambling on sporting events, not even the representatives of the commission who sould have known better and presumably had no special-interest axes to grind. Of the committee itself, only Congressman Mottl of Ohio seemed to understand the hypocrisy of the existing situation as he kept asking witness after witness how to counteract the massive corruption of the criminal justice system by the enormous power of illegal gambling interests supported by overwhelming public acceptance of betting.

The various arguments offered by opponents of legalized gambling reveal a great deal about the nature of the opposition. Analysis of them leads one to wonder why their position continues to prevail. Take first the testimony of those who represent the "national pastime." As far as gambling is concerned, baseball was indeed once the national pastime. Betting on baseball games was by far the largest portion of illegal gambling, with the World Series the single event that attracted the most action.

The popularity of baseball has fallen off greatly since those days, not in total numbers of audience, of course, but impressively in terms of proportion of attention paid by a nation of sports fans. Coincident with this fall from popularity has been a severe decline in the proportion of illegal gambling on baseball (though the World Series and championship playoffs do attract huge handles). There are, I think, two main reasons for this. Since the first expansion from two eight-team leagues, there has been a steady growth of imbalance between strong teams and weak, with proportionate growth in the odds assigned for individual games. Where 7–5 was once considered fairly long odds for a baseball game, now odds of 23–10 were not uncommon, making the whole proposition less attractive (just as the game itself grew unattractive for a majority of the schedule involving mediocre teams with diluted talent). Second, the movement in modern baseball toward reliance on relief pitchers has affected all serious baseball handicapping. Odds are primarily determined by rating the starting pitchers, and when they may be on hand less than two thirds of the game (on the average) the analysis becomes far more subject to the whims and unfathomable chance of the game (a game of fragmentary instants rather than inches, as good old Curt will probably babble on about another fifty years).

Can it be that the decline in baseball's relative popularity is directly due to its decline as a sporting proposition for the nation's bettors? In part? Baseball men would be the last to admit it. The spokesmen for this sport, the only major one in our time whose "world championship" has been fixed, are unanimous in stressing the integrity of the game. Baseball commissioner Bowie Kuhn, both in his statement before the Gambling Commission and his testimony before the House Select Committee on Professional Sports, is so perfectly an establishment figure that a cartoonist could not have invented a better one.

Acknowledging that the Black Sox scandal of 1919 was brought on by illegal gambling and that it forced creation of the position he occupies, Kuhn urges "put[ting] the heat on the enforcement people" to crack down on illegal gambling. He objects to "pool gambling" on professional sports (like the Delaware football lottery) because it would "open the door to other kinds of gambling." In his statement he confutes the four arguments he has heard in support of legalized gambling: (1) a blow to organized crime, (2) no adverse effects on society, (3) increased revenues, and (4) no irreparable harm to team sports.

On (1) he says that legalized gambling would stimulate the public demand for illegal gambling (as if the present enormous supply wasn't occasioned by present public demand), stimulate the "credit" and "rebates" services of bookies, and stimulate the illegal loan-shark opportunities. Kuhn's arguments here are based on his ignorance (genuine or feigned) of the volume of gambling (as in his reference to a "nongambling majority") and his assumption that legalized gambling would not offer attractive opportunities for bettors.

On (2) he calls gambling a "vice" and talks about its addictive nature and economic damage to lower income families. Such an argument presupposes that all betting is evil and that excessive or compulsive gambling is a norm. All evidence points to the opposite. On (3) he simply asserts that increased revenue would be modest and the human costs too high.

On (4) he is most elaborately vehement. Legalization would shake public confidence in the integrity of the game. Say it ain't so, Bowie. In support he cites reports of fixed games and attempted fixes in other sports in other countries where gambling is tolerated. He also cites an article in *Reader's Digest* concluding that "gambling presents a clear and present danger to professional team sports." Kuhn just won't acknowledge that the gambling exists because the people want it, that most people don't accept his pronouncement that it is a vice, and that whatever dangers there are exist quite totally exclusive of whether the gambling is legal or illegal. What legalization *would* do is force baseball to police itself far more rigorously than it would like; public scrutiny of legal betting would demand honest sporting events, while illegal gambling can only shudder and suffer silently at the possibility of dishonesty and is rendered virtually powerless by its underground nature to air questions in public.

For once the commissioner's position is supported by the players. According to Marvin Miller, executive director of the Major League Baseball Players Association, the association's executive board unanimously supported the opposition to legalized gambling and "the players were unanimously opposed." But according to Ed Garvey, executive director of the National Football League Players Association, his players "ended up with no posi-

tion" but "are taking a long look at it." Garvey at least acknowledges an awareness among the players of the great extent of betting on NFL games (just as the league does in its strict rules on
the reporting of injuries), but he said, "I guess if this were the
perfect world, there would not be any betting. . . ." Again the
cultural conditioning to an invalid moral stance is echoed.

The NFL commissioner Pete Rozelle has a more practical
reason for being "so terribly opposed" to legalized sports betting.
He argues that it would place an unnecessary extra burden of
pressure on the players. This reasoning seems inverted to me. If
the betting were open and aboveboard, suspicions could be aired
and likely allayed. No pressure in the direction of the integrity of
honest sport should be considered too great. Professional sports
should welcome such public pressure (even at the expense of
policing themselves with greater care), and the public should
demand it.

Rozelle was accompanied before the House committee by
two representatives of NFL management, Joe Robbie of the
Miami Dolphins and Bill Sullivan of the New England Patriots.
Robbie acknowledged the tremendous sums involved and argued
that giving it respectability is not going to relieve the threat it
poses by undermining confidence in the game. There was a kind
of pious repugnance in Robbie's final word on the issue: "I don't
want the gamblers close to the Orange Bowl." Sullivan's repul-
sion was stronger: he called legalized gambling a cancer that
should not be inflicted on the NFL. "I feel very strongly about
our game," he said, "that we haven't succeeded *because* of gambling; we have succeeded in spite of it."

The emotional conviction behind these words betray a discomfort with the truth as the evidence reveals it: pro football has
risen to pre-eminence among American sports fans in direct proportion to the rise of betting on pro football as the most popular
gamble going; the largest volume of betting occurs on the events
with the largest viewing audience; week after week the Monday
night game draws the heaviest handle, regardless of whether the

teams are contenders; the NFL Super Bowl is the biggest single bettable event in the country. Like it or not, the overwhelming commercial success and public acceptance of NFL football is nourished by its attractiveness as a sporting proposition, with betting lines or point-spreads established by professional odds-makers and then adjusted according to the public's response, almost as if it were a parimutuel operation, except that the handicap changes while the odds remain 11–10 and that there is only a 5-percent rake-off instead of the 14–18 percent at legal tote machines.

In parts of the Midwest, according to reliable reports, the biggest form of illegal gambling is college basketball. With some knowledge of this situation, no doubt, the coach of the 1976 NCAA champions from Indiana University recently lectured the COSIDA convention on how to attack gambling. Calling his suggestion "a great move forward for college athletics" he proposed that sports information directors boycott all publications that aid gamblers by publishing point-spreads or carrying gambling-related advertising. "I don't think people on the shadowy fringe of college athletics have any business being involved in what we're doing," says Bobby Knight, a brilliant coach whose ability to teach aggressively tight defense made his teams always competitive even when they didn't have talent of national-championship caliber. Knight is famous for his intensity and infamous for yanking freshman guard Jim Wisman off the court by his jersey after the kid committed two turnovers against Michigan (a wire-service photo of the move made most of the sports pages in the country). If "what we're doing" is inculcating a set of values in which college athletes are subjected to public humiliation and physical abuse by a coach whose winning record they have jeopardized by honest mistakes, then I think it's high time that the "shadowy fringe" be illuminated in public glare along with the opaque egomania of the win-crazed coach. We do not need ethical lessons taught by the Bobby Knights of the sports world.

Another kind of lesson comes from the testimony before the House committee by sports commentators, Leonard Koppett and

Red Smith of the *New York Times*, Dick Dozer of the *Chicago Tribune*, Bob Roesler of the *New Orleans Times Picayune*, and Howard Cosell of ABC. This panel of experts from the media was asked the familiar questions by Congressman Mottl. Koppett objected to legalized gambling because "sports pages would become very quickly simply tout sheets" and concluded, "I think it would have a very bad effect on the total picture of sports as it is presented to our society if gambling were legal." In other words, he was concerned not with the reality of the situation but with the *image* of the sports page, the image of the sportswriter, and the image of sports as the sports page projects it.

Dozer talked of the sports pages' inconsistent policies toward gambling. The *Chicago Tribune* once stopped printing results from out-of-town race tracks and was deluged with calls. The only possible reason for each caller was to know "how his bet came out with the bookie." The policy was quickly changed back. "The only reason we did was we would have lost tremendously in the circulation market. . . . It is too bad we have to say out of one side of our mouth gambling is terrible and yet out of the other side of the same mouth talk about the race results that we publish in our paper that would foster this very thing we are against." That's a pretty good working definition of hypocrisy. Dozer at least acknowledges the marketplace factor: gambling information is published because the public wants it—and the press acknowledges the public's right to know. But how does the idea that gambling is a terrible thing in itself come so readily to the lips of the president of the Baseball Writers Association?

Smith said he didn't quarrel with gambling on moral grounds but argued that "it is by its nature limited if it is underground, limited in volume." He thought that "the more we increase gambling, the greater is the danger of corruption in the sport." This position is partly the product of a great underestimation of the volume, which is excusable. But the logic by which illegality is a protection against corruption is hard to accept, especially from so worldly-wise a campaigner as Red Smith.

Roesler argued that legalized gambling wouldn't eliminate

the bookmaker, primarily on the evidence that certain forms of legalized gambling failed to take away the bookies' action. But since it has never (except in Nevada) been the same kind of action—the kind the people want—there is no way of measuring how much people are drawn to the bookmaker by the thrill of doing something illegal rather than the elemental desire for some action. "If you want to get rid of gambling," Roesler said, "have tougher law enforcement." But even if we chose up sides between the gamblers and the enforcers, there would be action. The police would probably have a pool on who got the most collars.

Cosell, to his credit, was silent on this issue.

A summary of the case against legalized gambling yields a curious design. The case is generally couched in emotional, moralistic terms, but the arguments are all in the pragmatic self-interest of the arguers. People in sports themselves, from owners to players, are jealous of their image of integrity, and they want to join the society at large in burying their heads away from the prospect of mass gambling as long as it can be freely done underground. They also want to avoid the expense and inconvenience of adequate self-policing and the specter of close official scrutiny (even licensing) of their operations and activity and personnel. The media are jealous of their images, too, and though they cynically report the news appropriate to gambling as a matter of marketplace necessity, they obsequiously accept the sports industry's pious premise that gambling is inherently evil.

Bureaucrats object that legalized gambling would create a massive new bureaucracy that would both defeat the revenue-producing purpose and provide inefficiency sufficient to reinforce patronization of illegal sources anyway. But why, as in the other arguments as well, need we assume that everything would be done in the worst possible way? If gambling were legalized, the opportunities for legitimate management in the private sector would be enormous. The gross handle could be taxed at a small (up to 2 percent) excise rate, and the net profits of course taxed as income.

On the other side, the only arguments for legalization come from law enforcement officials. They say simply that gambling should be legalized because antigambling laws are unenforceable—purely a matter of practicality. At least there is no appeal to morality here, but it would be well to examine across the board the priorities assigned by law enforcement agencies to gambling as opposed to fraud, to marijuana use as opposed to the poisoning of vital natural resources, to obscenity as opposed to protection of the public from violence and abuse. In other words, where ethical considerations ought to be brought to bear, there is often a cynical rationalization of practicality under the guise of "public morality" or "law" or "duty."

On his two visits to the classroom, Gerald Strine discussed some of these issues with me and my students. Strine reports on racing and sports gambling for the *Washington Post*, and he is apparently free of the self-serving hypocrisy that afflicts many of his colleagues. He dismisses the moralistic condemnation of betting by pointing out that "gambling equals speculation, the very basis of our capitalistic system." And then he wryly points out that there's "no onus if you win." Opprobrium is reserved for the losers, who then earn the designation of degenerates.

To the argument that legalized gambling would bring an undesirable element into the community, he said, "Nonsense," and about the threat of corruption, he suggested that it would be no greater, no less, than at present, except that the leagues would have to police it better. "Pete Rozelle doesn't have a big enough investigative staff to know what's going on anywhere." The gambling exists, he said, and the question is "what's the best way to live with it in order to let the greatest amount of the society enjoy it." Asked if this meant legal betting on sporting events, he said, "Absolutely—but not at the high school level. Let's not kid ourselves, college athletes are professionals as soon as they sign grants-in-aid."

Gerry Strine's remarks are most instructive on the subject of bookies and integrity. "The bookmaker will show you more trust than the First National Bank," he says, because his whole operation is built on trust. "He is the best safeguard to integrity in sport. The bookmaker wants to be sure of the integrity of what is being presented. What he fears is the crooked coach or the crooked athlete [or the crooked official]. What the bookmaker wants is to have the game played straight up. That's all the edge he needs, all the edge he wants." And that's why when it comes to the rare case of exposure of corruption it is when the "Justice Department operates on information received from bookies and gamblers, not from any investigative law enforcement agencies."

Strine's attitude makes perfectly good sense to me and is not, I think, the product of his own interest as a gambler (the Gambling Commission found that most bettors prefer to maintain the present illegal system) or as a writer of a regular column on sports gambling ("Playing Football" and "Playing Basketball"). Indeed, he seems to cut through the mass of hypocrisy that beclouds the subject. Nor is it necessary to justify gambling, as Felicia Campbell, chairperson of Nevada's Commission on the Status of People, has done, as offering many blessings to our society: an antidote to depression for many, a beneficial altered state of consciousness for many more, a saving sense of being human for prisoners, an interest in life for the elderly, an escape for working-class people, a quick fix of r-and-r for creative people. For excessive/compulsive behavior, she sensibly recommends investigation of the causes of the abnormality rather than condemnation of all related activities both normal and extreme.

Campbell's apologia for gambling is a useful corrective, but it should not be necessary. In a sports-oriented society where the main thrust of involvement is through spectation, gambling as a natural—perhaps inevitable—way of heightening the experience. It is a real as well as symbolic way of making the vicarious participation more direct. As I have said elsewhere, the best way to do this is with a bookie. The ethics of gambling are themselves as high-principled as the pure and purely abstract rules of any game, and they work best on football or basketball.

Here is the way it works. An independent expert or group,

taking all known factors into account (and sometimes computerizing them), rates a team against an opponent. Then the experts float a line or spread that indicates how many points, according to their form, the favorite should win by. This is adjusted, when necessary, according to early action or later developments or information. The idea is not to *predict* a margin of victory but to offer a sporting proposition that the public can accept on both sides. The public should assume that there is an equal chance with either team according to the point differential or handicap. Since the bookmaker wants to encourage betting on both sides, he works hard to establish a fair, accurate line. He succeeds best with an honest line that offers the most attractive sporting proposition. At its highest point of achievement, the system will yield a point-spread that makes every bet in doubt until the final gun or buzzer and every bettor "in" the game until the end. Fair play and honest competition are what is required here; the integrity of sport and the integrity of gambling, in a free and open system, would support and complement and guarantee each other.

# THE CONTAGION
# OF COMPETITION

The other institutions of our society have seen the strong hold sports have on the public mind, and they have tried in various ways to get a piece of the action. But co-option, as its prefix indicates, is not a one-way street. Sports have provided such attractive models of structure, organization, and systematic process that other institutions have sedulously borrowed from and servilely aped them until they themselves have become sportslike.

In some cases the similarities are so obvious that they have led to a variety of facile generalizations. Jack Higgs often points to a passage in Veblen's *Theory of the Leisure Class* which says that religion, sports, government, and warfare are always closely associated, as the four occupations of a predator culture and a leisure class. All show exemption from work. Higgs then remembers, as I do, the time in 1972 that Richard Nixon and Billy Graham met on Shield-Watkins Field in Neyland Stadium in Knoxville, Tennessee, to justify, support, and indeed sanctify the war in Southeast Asia. It was a memorable example of the unholy alliances Veblen had in mind, but by no means exceptional.

Every time a football game is preceded by the national anthem *and* an invocation as a military honor guard parades the colors, the same four-way shotgun wedding takes place. I once wrote a letter to the president of a state land-grant university, a famous educator and sports fan, and suggested that if there had to be an invocation before contests involving public institutions of higher education an invocation to the Muses would be appropriate. I even volunteered my services. The wily prexy foxily failed to answer.

My objection should not be mistaken for idiosyncratic whimsey. Many blacks for a couple of decades now have refused to stand for "The Star-Spangled Banner." One of my students expressed herself this way in her journal:

> Perhaps playing "The Star-Spangled Banner" at games is a way of incorporating it into our daily lives; an acknowledgment that a large number of Americans pay close attention to sports. I tend to see it as an underhanded government plot to promote patriotism. I don't like to be reminded of American capitalism when I go to a football game because I realize that American capitalism is what forced me to pay $12 for my seat.
>
> The only time I ever enjoyed hearing the national anthem played at a game was the year Jimi Hendrix played it at the World Series. The government must know how influenced Americans are by their sports heroes and figure they can cash in on this by making it look like all sports figures are really patriotic. Well, they can't fool us all the time because once in a while somebody like Duane Thomas comes along to embarrass them.
>
> Maybe hearing the anthem reduces the dissonance some people must feel when they show their enthusiasm for violent sports. Associating the violence of a hockey game with the American "spirit of competition" might make the violence seem justifiable. Playing the anthem may represent a blessing of the sport, condoning the violence.
>
> The importance of this argument is the extent to which we associate sports with patriotism and national pride. It is a phenomenon that not only the politicians and bureaucrats cash in on, but also team owners and the advertising industry.

There is a measure of cynicism here perhaps not warranted by the case, and it should be remembered that the relationship of sports to nationalistic feelings is hardly unique to the U.S.A. But the thrust of Patricia Ryan's comment is the notion of "cashing in." She seems to perceive an American society of ostentatious opportunism: if you've got something good, flaunt it; if you can make a buck on it, sell it; if you can avail yourself of something good, use it; if you see something good, get a piece of it.

The "using" of sports is not so clearcut an issue as some would have it. I could not say, as at least one Marxist critic does, that capitalism uses sports to perpetuate the rigid class structure and keep the masses down and entertained at the same time. This is not to say that sports may not have some such effect, because in general they do tend to strengthen the status quo, whatever the system happens to be. Nor is it to say that people will not try to use sports for their own benefit and that of their party or platform or persuasion. The point is that sports do as much as they are done to. They give as well as they get, or to put it more accurately they take and use as much as they get taken and are used.

The most crucial effect, as I see it, has nothing directly to do with conscious attempts at co-option. It is that when other institutions become sportslike they cease to function in a practical way with relation to the people. People become separated from their institutions when the institutions merely put on performances and act out *rituals* of involvement.

These are the social diseases of a jockocracy: confusion of roles, subversion of values, and distraction from the crucial issues of reality by the illusory significance of the mass-involving rituals.

William J. Bennett, a professor of law and philosophy at Boston University, recently wrote a defense of sports. Lumping together every kind of sports critic—from Jim Bouton to George Leonard, from Dan Jenkins to Jack Scott, from Russell Baker to Paul Hoch—in a distasteful mass of what he called "transcendental silliness, dime-store Marxism, and countercultural blather," he attacked all criticism on grounds none of the critics would recognize no less defend.

The *raison d'être* for Bennett's blast seems at times to be apolitical. He wants to boast, in an intellectual way of course, of his own athletic prowess as a member of a slow-pitch softball team, the Boston Flamingoes. (I sympathize with the impulse, having played for seven seasons on the might Knicks of Knoxville and once pitching a three-hit shut-out in league play—that's *slow*-pitch.) He is proud that he and his teammates take their games and themselves seriously. This is in contrast to their "occasional" opponents, whom they call the Cambridge Persons, who seem to enjoy playing around instead of playing the game to win. "We have more fun than the Persons," Bennett says. "We invest more in the game and the game is more of a release for us." But the real reason for the Flamingoes' pleasure, I think, is that they generally beat the Persons 28–3 or 21–0. If the game is so important and they take their fun so seriously, why ever would they play the Persons? Only to reinforce their superiority. The absolute value of playing is subordinated to the quantifiable value of winning—more runs, more fun.

Despite Bennett's disclaimers, insofar as he has a philosophical argument to pursue at all, it is a political one. And it is the politics of numbers. Bennett disdains the efforts of countercultural sports programs because they have failed, because "Americans have expressed more, not less, interest in a growing number of competitive athletics since the 'revolution' began, and if anything seem to be resisting the tendencies toward leveling in sports." He asserts that sports are "relatively unaffected by the general erosion of standards in the culture," and yet his own standards are entirely supported by numbers, by success in his terms, by winning—both games and majorities. He talks about excellence, but excellence is a measure of quality; Bennett deals in quantity, demonstrating what he refuses to acknowledge, that sports and other institutions feed upon each other's decline of standards and corruption of values.

Originally published in *Commentary*, Bennett's essay was reprinted in the *Washington Star* on February 15, 1976. On that very Sunday, at 1600 Pennsylvania Avenue, President Gerald

Ford was entertaining about 300 people at the Presidential Prayer Brunch for Professional Athletes. Eight of the guests ascended to the East Room podium and spoke intimately of their commitment to Christ—Miami Dolphin Norm Evans, runner Madeline Manning Jackson, Denver Bronco Calvin Jones, golfer Rik Massengale, tennis pro Dennis Ralston, soccer player Kyle Rote, Jr., figure skater Janet Lynn Solomon, and pitcher Jim Kaat. Washington Bullet Elvin Hayes said the invocation.

The president was gratified. When he spoke to his illustrious company, he confessed that he always read the sports pages in the newspapers first. He was no doubt further gratified when the story of the brunch got substantial attention on sports *and* front pages all over the country. Dick Schaap's report in the *Star* was page one, six columns across, just below the banner. The successful confounding of sports and religion, typified by membership of many of the president's guests in the Fellowship of Christian Athletes, was too good a thing for political neglect.

Examples may easily be multiplied. On a week end just before the Wisconsin primary last April, Ford was busy dedicating the Green Bay Packers Hall of Fame while Mo Udall was doing a campaign number in a basketball uniform in a Milwaukee Y. During the preceding basketball season, eager for any opportunity of getting national attention, Scoop Jackson showed up in the Washington Bullets locker room after a nationally televised game. The CBS camera was there, but Jackson, with his TV shirt and face on, couldn't get near the action. Oscar Robertson ignored him; Wes Unseld looked past him; Nick Weatherspoon and Len Robinson looked over him; Elvin Hayes glanced puzzledly at him and then turned away; Chenier and Riordan were hiding in the shower and the training room; worst of all, he never got on camera. For some reason I was moved at the pathos of the scene, though later I affected an ironic laugh at it. It wasn't the senator himself who was pathetic but the devaluation of the system that had led up to the whole charade.

No one seems to take exception to the conventional wisdom

that positive association with athletes means votes for politicians. To be perceived as an athlete is a strong appeal, a kind of de facto charisma. Barring that, friendship with and acceptance by athletes is the next best thing. Sonny Jurgensen on the stump for a candidate in suburban Virginia gives his conservative constituents something to cheer proudly for. Better yet, find an athlete with a modicum of political acumen—a Jack Kemp, a Vinegar Bend Mizell, or at one remove a John Glenn—and you've got an electable commodity. But these phenomena are innocuous enough in themselves; they may raise eyebrows or hackles but surely not the rabble.

Let us suppose, on the other hand, a less innocuous situation. Suppose that the whole political process has become a series of sports events. The two-party system is an easy analogue for team competition. The teams compete at every level and there is also competition among teammates for starting positions. In presidential elections, the teams become leagues, building through local and state caucuses, conventions, and primaries to the conference championship of the national convention, followed by the super bowl of the general election. The current proposal to hold a limited number of regional primaries is an idea the validity and viability of which are supplied by the playoff structure of professional sports and especially college basketball.

To give the events a sportslike *structure*, however, does not make them essentially sportslike. Yet it seems to me that if an emblem of contemporary American politics were to be emblazoned in heraldic terms it would be styled "fandom rampant on a public field." If the games of political competition are only metaphorically games, if the rituals of the elective process are only vaguely sportslike, it is nevertheless the case that they are perceived, enjoyed, and partaken by the masses of people in just the same way that sports are.

Except for the very few actively involved in framing issues and making policy—and more and more these tend to be image makers and purveyors rather than committed public servants, dedicated to a philosophical position or even a pragmatic ideal—the supporters of parties and their candidates are merely fans. They have pep rallies and cheerleaders and fundraisers, and if they contribute enough effort or money they get to mix with the players themselves. But they never get to contribute to policies or positions. They relate to political leaders, to the extent that they do, not to sympathetic, shared policies or programs or philosophies but simply in terms of "theirs" and "ours." They choose up sides, when there may be nothing to choose between the sides, because the choosing itself is an act of partisanship with which they are comfortable and familiar from their own rituals, games, and sports. The choice of token doesn't influence the outcome of Monopoly any more than the color of the uniform influences the result of a football game. The danger, then, is that the public will accept its role as fans in the political rituals (or as uninvolved spectators as many seem already to be) and thus remove itself from active participation in government. Our massive and perhaps unwieldy democracy will be a paternalistic government presumably *for* the people but neither *by* nor *of* the people. In a jockocracy, all the games are of the jocks, by the jocks, and presumably for the spectators.

In a political context, a nineteenth-century aphorist could say that religion was the opiate of the masses. Michael Novak has argued, with convincing conviction, that sport has become our religion. And the aphorism holds firm: sport is our people's super-drug—stimulant, depressant, tranquilizer, soporific all rolled up in one. But religion remains a more or less honored institution in our society, so that we cannot say it has been replaced by sports.

Religion exists side by side with sport, and in some ways hand in hand. The combination may seem odd, but the long and honorable tradition of muscular Christianity is just a comparatively recent version of the ancient intimacy between churchcraft and state-prowess. Robert Penn Warren has joked about Elijah competing in a superbowl of religion against the Philistine priests on Mount Carmel.

It is not my intention here to examine critically such institutions as the Ys and the Fellowship of Christian Athletes, any more than I would presume to criticize the Mormons on the PGA tour for tithing their prize winnings. It may seem incongruous for clergymen to invoke a basically gentle and noncombative deity in blessing a football game, but if I disapprove on grounds of taste or logic it is not a moral judgment. Perhaps it should be. In practice, at least, the Fellowship of Christian Athletes has provided many competitors who are notoriously unsportsmanlike with a vaguely defined and loosely embraced rationale for the way they live and act. Still, I cannot condemn a principle of faith because of whole-sale abuses by the "faithful."

Nor am I appalled at the ludicrous apparition of nuns playing soccer, ministers leading grass drills, and rabbis organizing volley-ball leagues. These seem to me the desperate measures of institu-tions grasping at gimmicky straws to simulate a relevance in the hopes of salvaging some interest if not souls. And they seem almost as trivial as the stereotyped golfing priest (a character we some-times conceive of as having been invented by J. F. Powers). Or the story about the black American soldiers in Rome:

Who that man?
That the pope.
What he say?
He blessin' the crowd.
What he do?
He preparin' to shoot a free throw.

No, what does concern me is the kind of subversion of values I see when religious proselytizers perform as if in competition with other beliefs, when preachers are indistinguishable in style and language and rhetoric from cheerleaders and exhortatory coaches and political demagogues, and when the muscular-Christian types epitomized by Elmer Gantry flex their bulges in the service of self and the exercise of power. I can see only a confusion of values in the idea of a professional athletic team having a chaplain to lead regular prayers before and after games. For the performance of the sport it is as meaningless as wearing the same dirty socks and running on the field in the same order—a matter of pure form with no substance. For the practice of religion it is as meaningless as the slurred grace in a language the diners don't know. There needs to be a present-day Cardinal Newman to say, "If there be a God, since there is a God, He cannot concern Himself with the score of a game."

There are some who say that twentieth-century America's religion is not sport but sex. It might be better to say that the two go together. Certainly our society has developed a commitment to physical well-being so strong that it is nearly a universal cult with us. The quest for creature comforts, that inescapable application of "the pursuit of happiness" in the contemporary American dream, is an essential part of this cult but by no means the only one. The quest for perfect health is another, and we have learned en masse that excessive comfort often takes a heavy toll in physical fitness. Feeling good requires more than goods and more than the patent panaceas for bodily ills and stresses. There can be no genuine comfort for a creature whose body is not sound. Thus, the goal of universal participation in some kind of athletic activity has become a desideratum alongside universal literacy. Sex has its place in this picture, too, both as an element of physical fitness and as a function of emotional soundness.

A young graduate student of my acquaintance in the sixties brought home to this naïve professor some surprising truths. I had thought of her as a typical, traditional pre-professional student of literature, the type that thinks a phallus is a phallic symbol. For some reason, call it foolish stereotyping, I was surprised to learn that she ran every day. I don't mean gentle jogging. She ran in earnest on the university track.

I asked her why, and she was surprised I asked. Her body was important to her, she said, and she had to stay in shape to feel right. The only ways she knew to stay in shape, she said, were running, swimming, and fucking. It was neither the word nor the uncalled-for intimacy that shocked me. It was the total naturalness, the complete absence of anything that could be called "prurient interest." Here was an expression of a whole generation, mainstream young America in the sixties, that believed in feeling good about being in touch with their bodies.

It was shortly after this lesson that I first heard the word "sportfucking" in the Paul Mazursky film, *Blume in Love*. It was used by a psychiatrist who prescribed it to Blume as a remedy for his agony over losing his wife to divorce. A healthy body, and presumably a healthy attitude toward it, would provide for a healthier psyche. Blume wasn't ready either for the word or the concept, but even in the comic context it was beginning to make sense to me.

A genuine revolution had taken place in attitudes, a revaluation as striking as any in the history of ideas. Before the change, physical activity associated with sport was considered good clean fun and encouraged in public, but physical activity associated with sex was shunned in public and only sanctioned at all under collateral conditions of emotional and spiritual and legal and even religious requirements. After the change, all these restrictions are removed. Sexual activity is regarded as another form of good clean fun and except for the most intimate acts is permissible in public. What once could not be mentioned in polite society is now seen and done. It is not a matter of complete sexual freedom, by any means, but it is at least an acknowledgment that sex can be enjoyed as a purely physical, even athletic activity.

A number of factors have contributed to this phenomenal shift in values. One is a peripheral issue of the Freudian revolution of sensibilities, wherein all sports are perceived as sublimated sexual activity. If the clean and innocent fun is just a mask for the dark and shameful secrets, then maybe those private acts aren't so bad after all. When the unmasking takes place, when the burden of guilt is removed from sexual acts, then sex could come out of the closet (and eventually even minority sexual preferences) and enter the living and family rooms alongside sports. To a degree sex might replace sport since the necessity for sublimated sexual activity was lessened if not erased. But as it happens, the lessening of sexual repression has been accompanied by increased athletic activity in a way that makes any direct correlation hard to find. Perhaps the new license for physical expression could account for increased activity on all physical fronts (as it were).

A local radio talk-show host, a little man with a big voice and bigger ego problems, once put it to me on the air that the urge to compete athletically is just a male way of showing off for the females, a kind of ritual mating- or courting-show. (He is forever "putting it to" someone in a way that might suggest an appropriate Freudian interpretation of his choice of phrasing.) Nonathletes often exaggerate the childlike aspect of sports, and this seems to me a particularly childish way of doing so. Unfortunately the Freudian revolution has given rise to any number of half-assed theories about human behavior. This particular assertion, while it may accurately describe an occasional performer or performance, accounts for no general observation that can be made about sports phenomena, even if we set aside the phenomenal growth of women's athletic participation and isolated the men.

Another factor is the evolving customs of social dancing. One of the most ancient of art forms in virtually all cultures, the dance may often mirror a society's values in both substantive and formal terms. While traditional dances record, commemorate, and preserve a kind of cultural ancient history, new dances celebrate changing mores. The close relation of sport and dance has often been noted. Exercises in the martial arts and gymnastics, both oriental and occidental, are as nearly dance as sport; the balletic moves of basketball and soccer players (to take just two of many possible examples) are dutifully reported by the media; Knute Rockne is inspired by a nightclub dance routine to the Notre Dame shift; Ali dances in the ring (Sugar Ray danced in the ring and on stage too); Nijinsky and Villella and Gene Kelly are praised as fine athletes; etc.

Recent generations have seen spectacular changes in social

dancing. Rigid Victorian restrictions about contact and distance gave way to permissiveness in both respects, and dancing became a vehicle for undisguised public sexual activity. Almost simultaneously it became more vigorously athletic. Dance bands regularly alternated slow (sexy) and fast (sporty) numbers in their sets, from the tango to the Charleston, from the foxtrot to the jitterbug. Then came the move toward freer individual expression—a further loss of restrictiveness though apparently a de-sexing—and in its wake a reawakening of the impulse to group dancing. At present what we see is a coming together of the sex and sport elements: bump, boogie, and hustle all have their share of coupling, athleticism, free expression, and integrated motion. Dance, then, shows in its own way both the new emphasis on physical activity and the new freedom for sexual activity. Dancing is sportfucking, once removed but to music.

Once it becomes commonly accepted that sex is both natural and healthy in a society that has long preached physical fitness and athletic participation, the idea of playing at sex has been firmly implanted. But as I have said in many another context, influences move in both directions across points of contact. Sport and dance reflect each other. Sex invades the general category of sport, and sport invades the attitudes and practices of sex.

Sex handbooks are multiplied in the form of coaches' (called counselors) recommendations for training, preparation, strategy, and performance. Sex becomes a team sport with varying numbers of participants. Circuits are organized and clubs and leagues and schedules and arenas. There are published records of results, the best performers rise to challenges and advance to a higher level of competition, professionalism becomes common along with its common byproducts of rating by dollar signs and increased spectation. Ironically the growth of permissiveness in participation or performance brings with it a growth in surrogate participation, voyeurism, and even impotence, just as the tremendous growth in athletic skills at the apex of the performance pyramid is accompanied by a decrease in competence among the mass at the base. The distance between the jock and the athletic supporter is stretched wider and wider past any vestige of elasticity.

In the sex-as-sport syndrome the most striking phenomena are the compilations of statistics. As I have said before, the sporting, competitive urge that so moves us is nowhere evidenced so clearly as in our predilection for records. We tabulate our sports-mindedness in every way, and the tables extend into virtually every area of reportage. Not only our sports pages but the whole omnibus of our awareness is one big *Guiness Book of World Records*. Somehow, as the quantification of values proceeds in all areas, the sense of measuring performance in competition becomes a compulsion. In matters of sex we are given both scales of normalcy and standards of proficiency to measure ourselves by. There may come a time when to the number of chin-ups and the clocking over an obstacle course on our physical fitness records will be added the frequency and duration of orgasms.

As an institution the press probably has a more intimate relationship with sport than any other. Surely the way in which we perceive sports, including the amassing of statistics, depends in large part on the press. The press, in turn, depends in large part on sports to furnish material and audience. That Golden Age we hear so much about was also a golden age for the ability of sports entrepreneurs to manipulate the press. Tex Rickard promoted prize fights and pro sports into seven-figure events by lavishing creature comforts and good stories on the press. Even when he locked reporters out of the Carpentier camp because he knew that anyone who saw the Frenchman would know he had no chance against Dempsey, Rickard planted stories of secret strategy and mystery punches. And it was also a golden age of sports reporting à la Grantland Rice, who never said anything bad about anyone.

Interviewing George Solomon and Bill Tanton, sports editors respectively of the *Washington Post* and *Baltimore Evening Sun*, in my class, I suggested that there was little difference between a Rickard and a Don King in their ability to handle the press. But of course special events like heavyweight championship fights occupy a very small percentage of the column inches devoted to sports, and most contemporary sportswriters have abjured the Rice school of sweetness and pap.

"It's not our function to make people happy," Solomon said. "We're not the toy section or the comic section" but a section made up of professional reporters. Tanton suggested that sportswriters became reporters, in part, because the rise of the electronic media meant that the print media had to take on a dimension of thorough analysis to compete at all. "And I resent the suggestion," he said, "that we are shills for teams and are any less professional than cityside reporters."

To a certain extent things are as they have long been, with management offering food, tickets, booze, travel arrangements, and even money bonuses for sympathetic coverage, and withholding privileges because of critical coverage. But in large part the excesses and egregious abuses have been removed from what was once a sickening, mutually parasitic relationship. Solomon noted that the national association of sports reporters honors the commandment "Thou shalt not take anything." And it is not likely that an owner like Bob Short will ever again be able to order an announcer like Shelby Whitfield to say over the air that the weather is beautiful at the ballpark when there is a high likelihood that a game will be rained out.

It may be that alone of our major institutions the press and its values are not being progressively subverted or eroded by the jockocracy. One aspect of media coverage, however, that should be called in question is the massive conversion of ex-athletes to TV commentators. Pat Summerall discussed this during his visit to the classroom, very frankly regretting the practice. He suggested that he and his usual partner, Tom Brookshier, were exceptions to the rule in that they served a long apprenticeship before they could consider themselves professional broadcasters.

He talked about the difficult adjustment and his dissatisfaction with his performance for the first few years. In time he improved to the point where he considers himself professionally competent (most rate him among the best in the field). He said,

> I'd been lucky enough to play in New York with the Giants, in the communications capital, and the Giants were good in those years so that a lot of us were in demand at that time. And I think because of that the network was more patient with me than they would be today. In fact, today I might not get a shot at all.

There is something most revealing in this refreshingly candid account. It is an acknowledgment of how the value of winning on an athletic field carries over in a presumption of "winning" in quite another field. Our society is saturated with such presumptive transvaluations.

Two more institutions, pillars of our civilization, remain to be examined briefly in this context, with one more reserved in detail for the following chapter. On the subject of sports and medicine, my guest was Stanford Lavine, orthopedic surgeon, team doctor for the Bullets, the Redskins, and the University of Maryland teams, and once quarterback for the Terrapins on a winning Gator Bowl team. Dr. Lavine was very positive about the advances being made in the field of sports medicine. He was even optimistic about the care of injured athletes and the control of drug abuse. He made a very convincing case that medicine has not only not been corrupted by sports values but has contributed to the integrity of athletics and the protection of athletes.

Unfortunately not all the practitioners in the field, licensed and otherwise, are Stan Lavines. Three football players who heard him wrote differently in their journals out of their own experiences. One was openly cynical:

> Almost all the ball players take speed before games and if a player is hurt the big man just tells Doc to shoot him up and let him play— they worry about injury after we win or lose. The one really big gripe I have is that if you are hurt and you cannot help the program

any more the coaching staff will do anything in their power to get you to quit so they have your scholarship to give to someone else.

Another sadly commented on medical practices as a sign of overemphasis in college athletics:

> Judging only from my own experiences I would strongly disagree with someone who says that college athletics are not overemphasized. From my past dealing as a football player I have seen too many players inserted back into the lineup without proper time to heal their various wounds and injuries.

The third betrayed only a trace of irony in his straightforward observation:

> It's nice to know that Dr. Lavine's first responsibility is to the good of the players on the team because I know that all doctors don't feel that way, although they may say they do. A lot of doctors will go against their will if the coach says he wants a certain player ready by game day. The doctor is then under pressure, so he will shoot him up if he has to.

In general the conclusion of the athletes seems to be that the value of winning has often caused the Hippocratic oath to be outshouted by the coaches and fans calling for the old college try.

Any discussion of contemporary sports must necessarily be involved in legal matters. Sports pages are filled with discussions of litigation, legislation, arbitration, contract disputes, strikes, and the like. Hypothetically, the phrase "The Oscar Robertson Game" would be a title for a study of contemporary basketball, yet the phrase "The Oscar Robertson Case" refers to a proceeding at law that is of far-reaching practical significance to contemporary sport.

I asked Donald Dell, former Davis Cup player and captain, now an attorney involved primarily in the representation of professional athletes, whether he thought the courts were the right place to bring about changes and reforms in sports. He thought not, preferring the collective bargaining and negotiating processes. Nor did he see legislation as a remedy for the ills of professional sports, reminding us that historically legislation has limited the freedom of an open-marketplace situation by creating exemptions for owners and leagues. He is a proponent of contracts negotiated with integrity and honored on both sides. Thus, while he opposes renegotiation as a matter of principle, he realizes that in practice the players are often poorly advised and bargain from a position of weakness because of the absence of competitive bidding.

Dell agreed with me that there is a natural relationship between sports and the law. He noted the case of Julius Erving, for which he agreed to serve as arbitrator. When he withdrew from the proceeding, his successor was Archibald Cox, who in turn withdrew to accept the position of special prosecutor. "Do you mean," I asked, "he dropped Dr. J. for Watergate? Where are his priorities?" Ironically, Dell observed, the case was decided not by any judicial proceeding but by dollars.

If adequate counsel was important, I wondered if he thought that athletes should be represented by agents when they negotiated their four- or five-year deals with colleges. He thought not, because he felt that the distinctions between amateur and professional were important, but he hoped that young athletes would be well advised by family and friends. He did not take seriously what I recognized as a trend which would lead eventually to legal counsel for the talented eight-year-old as he enters the Little League Draft.

But all this has to do with what I have called a "natural relationship." It is the law dealing with matters of sport and in some cases bringing about changes in athletic institutions, changes that are more likely than not to be for the good. What really concerns me is the institution of the law being touched, that is, tainted, and moved, that is, subverted, by the jockocracy.

I submitted to Donald Dell the notion that the law, the

American legal system, has come more and more to be a sport. It is an adversary system set up to be played in public as a spectacle with spectators and an umpire and a set of rules and a compendium of records called precedents. And I supposed that something very important about us, about our society, is reflected in this identity.

He concurred substantially with the proposition, saying in part, "It's all hell-bent to winning or losing. There is a tremendous competitive-success-winning/losing syndrome in our society which we embrace from about the age of five." A student picked up the subject and asked, "How do you feel when you lose a case?" He said, "Terrible. It's absolutely like a physical contest" and went on to say that one reason he went into trial law initially was because it was, like tennis, a one-on-one contest.

The one exception Dell took to what he called my "analogy" was that the stakes were different. But it seems to me that in the long run the stakes become the same. With the emphasis on winning within the rules of the game, a judicial system loses sight both of abstract principles of justice and also of the real humanity of the people involved in matters at law. The latter are players, and perhaps minor ones, in the game; the former are irrelevant to the proceedings though they may have been the purpose for which the game was organized.

Once again the values inherent in the substance of the game itself have been subordinated to the values of maintaining the empty structure for the playing. And so even proceedings at the bar, which are of genuine innate concern to individual people, become spectator sports in which the people have no real part.

# VIII

# THE GRAVES
# OF ACADEME

In an irony of monumental proportions, the American institution that is one of the chief benefactors of the jockocracy is also one of its chief victims—the educational system. The following discussion will focus on higher education, but it should be understood that secondary and even primary schools reflect the subversion of values that has taken place in colleges and universities.

To begin this discussion, I would defend the presence of athletics in the academy as acceptable, appropriate, and desirable. This premise is solidly based both in definition and tradition. If the purpose of higher education is to develop not just some narrowly restricted and highly specialized abilities but the complete person, fully integrated within himself as a requisite for full integration in society whether or not in a position of leadership, then the individual's body cannot be neglected by any institution or individual attempting to fulfill that purpose.

The Greek ideal of the whole man, reduced with effective oversimplification into the Roman slogan *mens sana in corpore sano*, stands at the heart of our philosophy of education. It is instructive, then, to look briefly at how that ideal has suffered in practice in Greece, in Rome, and—closer to home—in the British Empire.

A great deal of attention, care, expense, and effort went into the public concern for the athlete in Greece. The building of a stadium was perhaps second in significance only to the building of a temple. In fact, the closeness of athletic competition to religion must be recognized. It was an intimate relationship. Games were held to celebrate festivals throughout the religious calendar, not just once every four years. The winning of athletic laurels was as great an honor as the winning of ivy crowns for artistic achievement, also a matter of commemorating the gods. Isocrates said that the "twin arts of gymnastics and philosophy are parallel and complementary, by which their masters prepare the mind to become more intelligent and the body more serviceable, not by sharply separating the two kinds of education but by using similar methods of instruction, exercise, and discipline."

But the athletes themselves were less and less likely to be "whole persons," skilled young men with the background and training of philosopher-kings. And they became less and less likely even to be drawn from the patrician class. They were specialists, like the actors and the priests, isolated from even the possibility of broad, liberal development that was the ideal.

When you see the facilities devoted to the care of the athletic performer, the finely appointed chambers where they received their perfumed rubdowns from slaves with velvet gloves, you must be struck by the splendor of the athlete's status. Yet the more profound impression is that of the isolation of the sacrosanct.

The Greeks tended to idolize their athletes. They deified them. And there is a very fine line between deification and dehumanization. The practice totally inverted the ideal, and the Greeks wound up with a professionalized, ghettoized, depersonalized breed of athletes. It was a startling progression, but not an unnatural one, from the glorious youths—amateur athletes in the purest form—for whom Pindar composed his paeans, to the breed of athletes execrated by Euripides as the worst of the "myriad afflictions that beset Hellas" (tr. Moses Hadas).

In latter-day Rome, of course, the practice was even worse than the corrupted practices of professional boxers and charioteers in Greek amphitheaters and circuses. The concept of athlete as gladiator is a thorough corruption of the Apollo Agonistes figure. Instead of the gods being glorified by the spectacle and achievements of competition and competitors, who thereby attain a god-like status themselves, we have a ruling class glorified and amused. Or disgusted, as by the spectacle of female athletes that aroused Juvenal's scalding scorn and ridicule in his sixth Satire. The spectacles have been devalued, to the degree that the drama's aesthetic shock of recognition or reversal of intention (Aristotle's *peripeteia*) has become the cheap thrills of an entertainment like *Jaws* or *The Exorcist*. The athletes are special, but they are slaves, dehumanized rather than deified, in the manner of prize bulls, dancing bears, or fighting Bantam roosters.

As the Renaissance brought to Western Europe the re-emerging concepts of classical ideals, it was not the corrupted practices of the ancients that were found appealing or even examined. Rather there was a conscious attempt to find points of identity between evolving codes of noble behavior in the West and the rediscovered Hellenic ideals. Germanic and Celtic leaders, at least as they are revealed to us in the literatures, were expected to be the very models of Platonic philosopher-kings: graced with physical, mental, spiritual, and social abilities; healers, poets, warriors, philanthropists, priests, shamans, judges, and smiths all in one.

The chivalric code passed down to patrician English education partakes of all these sources. Before we jump to the playing fields of Eton and West Point, let us look at two curricular models of that code that were strong influences on the educated Englishman and, more to the point, the English educator. One is found in an unlikely place, lines from the Prologue to Chaucer's *Canterbury Tales*, where in the combined figures of the Knight and his son, the Squire, we are given a composite icon of what a good, well-rounded nobleman should have and know: warcraft and honor, religious humility and loyal pride, music and poetry, horsemanship and martial arts, love and tradition, a sense of decorum in all things and in all actions an effective body language.

The other model is Castiglione's *Courtier*, the early sixteenth-century Italian handbook on how to be the perfect gentleman. It was so much in vogue in England that it made required-reading lists at Oxford and Cambridge and so popular that anyone who had pretensions to courtliness in mid-century England had read it in Italian or English or both. Castiglione's curricular requirements include the martial and equestrian arts, field events, tennis, and "to know how to swim, to leap, to run, to throw stones." But, perhaps with the examples of corruption in antiquity in mind, he says,

> Our Courtier having once become more than fairly expert in these exercises, I think he should leave the others on one side: such as turning summersaults, rope-walking, and the like, which savour of the mountebank and little befit a gentleman.

The problem in England, as it had been in earlier societies and as it was to be in America, was that the ideal was applicable—if practicable at all—only among a small ruling aristocracy. It would indeed be difficult to argue that what was especially beneficial and desirable to a whole society—the development of the whole man—must be restricted to a few, or that a society, having accepted a model for excellence, would sacrifice universal or egalitarian instincts and aspirations so that a select number might achieve that excellence.

Toynbee found it significant that "organized games and other sports should have come into fashion simultaneously with the rise of Industrialism" and spread "with Industrialism from England over the World." He saw sports as attempts at " 'recreation' from the soul-destroying exaggeration of the Division of Labour which the Industrial System of economy entails." Sports, like the rigorous celebration of the Sabbath, were ways of re-establishing the integrity of human selves. But in modern times,

> this attempt to adjust Life to Industrialism through Sport has been partially defeated because the spirit and the rhythm of Industrialism have become so insistent and so pervasive that they have invaded and infected Sport itself. . . . In the Western World of today professional athletes—more narrowly specialized and more extravagantly paid than the most consummate industrial technicians—now vie with the professional entertainers in providing us with horrifying examples of

the concentration of energies on a particular technique at the expense of well-rounded development as an integral member of society.

Toynbee goes on to describe three disconcerting images: an English football field at Sheffield where the grass was being kept artificially green by tapping the municipal water supply at the parched end of summer; an American collegiate football field with floodlights so that "football-players might be manufactured there by night as well as day" like factories with continuous shifts; and another American field roofed over so that "practice might go on whatever the weather," erected at "a fabulous sum" with beds ranged round the sides "for the reception of exhausted or wounded warriors." He was informed that the players constituted only a small fraction of the student body and approached competition with "the same grim apprehension as their elder brothers had felt" going into battle. He concludes,

> In truth this Anglo-Saxon football was not a game at all. It was the Industrial System celebrating a triumph over its vanquished antidote, Sport, by masquerading in its guise.

Apologists for and rationalizers of the presence of athletics in American higher education do not accept Toynbee's notion of sport as antidote to the economic system. They see one as an integral part of the other. They acknowledge both the community's needs to recreate and the individual's need to integrate a whole human self. Yet they have been powerless to prevent the professionalism in amateur sport, overspecialization of the particular rather than integration of the whole, dehumanization and classist identification. In short, the precipitous decline from the ideal experienced in Greece, in Rome, and in Western Europe has been recapitulated. At the same time, Wellington's slogan ("The battle of Waterloo was won on the playing fields of Eton"), which had little sense when coined by the duke in his dotage, but was honored in theory and given new currency when General MacArthur revised it for West Point, has come to have less and less applicability to contemporary conditions.

Illustrious, forceful, and influential leaders have fostered the ideal, even in the face of contradictory experience. For my few examples here I will take Teddy Roosevelt, J. F. Kennedy, and Byron White. And I would agree in theory with parts of their position, though I cannot always stomach the rhetoric or the frames of reference. In "Value of an Athletic Training," T. R. deplored tendencies toward brutality that had crept into our athletics, but he strongly advocated the strengthening of virtues "developed by . . . playing the rougher and manlier sports, especially outdoor sports." He discounted the value of professional sports except insofar as they excite spectators to emulate the performances, because he saw regular exercise to "tone both body and mind" as a way to "offset the evil consequences of a merely sedentary occupation." The Rough Rider supposed that it

> would be an ill thing for this republic if we developed on the lines of the Byzantine and Bengalese if our mercantile men learned nothing but how to make money and our lawyers, students, and men of trained intellects generally, grew to unite "the heads of professors with the hearts of hares."

He then focused his attention on colleges, offering the following arguments in defense of athletics: (1) People who object to sports because they do not "make men succeed better in after-life" could say the same of "classics and mathematics, philosophy, history, and modern languages." (2) Sports, like lectures and recitations, have positive indirect effect on boys' character. (3) As a group, students who are athletes have a higher scholastic average than a group of all nonathletes. (4) Men "who take part in vigorous sports . . . are apt in after-life to do rather better in the rough work of the world." (5) Sports tend to minimize dissipation.

Setting aside the sexist bias and the bully bluster, one finds here the traditional, classical thinking about the whole man. "Far above bodily strength, far above mere learning," said T. R., "comes character" and the training of body as well as intellect contributes thereto. These are sentiments we hear echoed still, and to give Teddy's analysis full credit, he also saw the "real danger" in the "exaggerated regard felt by the public generally for the athletic hero of the moment." What he saw, however, was the danger to the individual rather than to the values of the society in which such exaggerations have profound causes and effects.

The better part of a century later, in 1961, President Kennedy addressed the National Football Foundation and Hall of Fame, sounding some of the same notes. Indeed he quoted Theodore Roosevelt as he sounded the call for remedying the physical deficiencies found in the American population at large. He quoted Thomas Jefferson, too—"Not less than two hours a day should be devoted to exercise"—appropriately enough in a context in which he said,

> I do not suggest that physical development is the central object of life, or that we should permit cultural and intellectual values to be diminished, but I do suggest that physical health and vitality constitute an essential element of a vigorous American community.

For our discussion here, Kennedy's two most significant models were men who exemplified T.R.'s ideals: Barry Wood, a ten-letter man at Harvard and also the first marshal of Phi Beta Kappa, who "since then has combined a life of leadership in the medical profession," and Byron White, then deputy attorney general, "who was simultaneously a Rhodes Scholar and a halfback for the Detroit Lions, and the year that he led the league in ground gained rushing, was also number one man in his class at the Yale Law School." These demonstrated the capacity and Kennedy urged the necessity of combining "intellectual energy and physical vitality."

Four years later Whizzer White, by then an associate justice of the United States Supreme Court, addressed the National Federation of State High School Athletic Associations in similar sentiment though with loftier and more erudite associations. He did, however, quote President Kennedy on "what the Greeks knew: that intelligence and skill can only function at the peak of their capacity when the body is healthy and strong; that hardy spirits and tough minds usually inhabit sound bodies."

White judiciously went to the heart of the problem. Accepting the philosophical premise that "schools should concern themselves with the body as well as the mind" on the pragmatic basis that "it is the schools who have the only really consistent access to our youth and, if room for recreation is not available in the schools, it will not be available at all," he goes on to question "the validity of our existing athletic system." He presents concisely the argument that

a physical fitness program can produce a strong and healthy youth without the elaborate overlay of competitive athletics on an interscholastic basis. The system of school against school, it is said, inevitably has unfortunate consequences for a truly comprehensive program: energy and effort are concentrated upon producing the school team; it is an exclusive system which leaves all but the chosen few sitting in the grandstands to cheer; the participants themselves are so pressured into peak performance and pushed to such limits that they neglect their minds and overtax their bodies, the very antithesis of a sound program. Moreover, if these unfortunate conditions exist in the high schools, it is said that the colleges are even worse, much worse.

In White's view, history should have taught us that "athletics carry the seeds of their own destruction." And though no one can justify a program that benefits only the few and neglects the many or a system that discourages those who cannot compete with the best from competing at all, it does not follow that schools must choose between the school team on one hand and no athletic or physical fitness programs on the other:

> There is no incompatibility between a broadly focused physical education program and the team sports. There is no necessity to discard either. On the contrary, there is ample justification for both. Such a program presents few problems that able management and direction cannot cure, particularly when it is tied to the schools, which have the responsibility of producing whole men and women who are stunted in neither mind nor body, who are neither mental nor physical cripples and who must be willing and able to face the rigors of the future.

But where is one to find the ideal management to put into practice the ideals shared by so many thinkers on the subject? It is much easier to find examples of the unconsciously suicidal tendencies referred to by Justice White. And we need not look to ancient history; our evidence stands before us in the ivied traditions of American collegiate athletics.

At the end of the last and the beginning of this century, our campuses sustained a legacy of pure sport and amateurism inherited from English models. College men competed in the pursuit of excellence, mostly in loose club arrangements and often without any official sanction and sometimes by associating with off-campus institutions like Ys and Athletic Clubs. There were baseball and cricket, football and rugby, crew and wrestling, boxing and lacrosse, ice hockey and field hockey, among many. Intercollegiate competition emerged as naturally as water and cream seek their own levels, and it is a fact worthy of attention that clubs or teams had captains first and then managers and not for a long time coaches and not for a longer time paid, professional coaches.

When James Naismith invented basketball in 1891, at a school for training YMCA staffers, for the purpose of providing healthy, sporting, competitive activity between outdoor seasons, he saw and intended the game as the kind of pure recreation in which a ball would be thrown up and people would just play with it. He was gratified that at first it worked just that way, both for men and women, but it could not last. At the University of Kansas, where he spent most of his later years, it was with an amusement not without irony that Coach Phog Allen used to say that Naismith may have invented basketball but Allen invented basketball coaching. With organized intercollegiate competition came official structuring and a professionalization that begins with salaried coaches. Naismith was dismayed by the developments, but Allen, who for a while coached three college teams at the same time, pioneered the promotional potential of the sport in such directions as Olympic competition, national tournaments, and organizational professionalism.

Allen eventually was surpassed as the winningest coach by a former player of his, Adolph Rupp. In Coach Rupp's devotion to basketball may be seen the degree of divergence both from Naismith's idea of a recreational game and from the idea of collegiate sport providing a sound body for a sound mind in the development of an integrated self. It was Rupp who refused to allow Artur Rubinstein to practice where he was to give a concert on the campus of a great state land-grant institution because it might interfere with his basketball team's practice.

This kind of disintegration of values may be seen even more clearly in the case of the coach who surpassed Rupp as the winner of the most national titles on his way to unprecedented records and a reputation for fineness and wisdom—John Wooden. It was John Wooden who could never allow such matters as the politics, legal problems, scholastic difficulties, or social principles of his players to interfere with his relationships with them as their basketball coach. In one memorable instance, he denied some players' request to make a mild protest gesture in support of a Yale athlete (victim of a mindless bureaucratic action), not because he disagreed philosophically with their position—he never confronted the issue—but because he couldn't understand how his student-athletes could concern themselves with any problem but how to win their next game.

College basketball coaches, however egomaniacal as a group they may seem to be (Shirley Povich has called them as a group "the worst element in sports, in my experience, in point of self-aggrandizement and selfish procedures and ego building"), can hardly be accused of being the root of the problem. They are rather a symptom than a cause of the process by which amateur athletics changes to professionalized entertainment, a process that is not exclusive to the universities. Nor is it a process exclusive to the class of patrician amateurs who won their varsity letters on our campuses two or three generations ago.

The plebeian game of baseball, that monument to egalitarian, rural (if not pastoral) America, was professionalized early on. But as long as social and demographic conditions allowed, it continued to be the game played by all American boys. At the same time, in its professionalized form (organized leagues, barnstorming troupes, and local teams drawing salaries to represent the old home town or its industries), it soon became a vehicle for upward mobility by immigrant, ethnic youths. The narrator of E. L. Doctorow's *Ragtime*, watching the Giants of McGraw, Marquard, Merkle, Doyle, Meyers, Snodgrass, and Herzog play a Boston team with Cocrehan, Moran, Hess, and Rudolph, is "led inevitably to the conclusion that professional baseball was played by immigrants."

Ironically from the perspective of the game today, it was football that, of our major sports, maintained the heritage of pure amateurism among the patrician institutions of the Northeast.

While recruiting began at least as early as 1901 when Fielding Yost brought Willie Heston with him to Michigan from the West Coast, college football remained remarkably free of professionalism even when the balance of power shifted from the Ivies to the Big Ten. Though coaches were hired by college presidents and salaried by the universities, they themselves were scholars more often than not and their charges always were.

The change began clearly to be perceived sometime in the twenties, the Golden Age of Sport, which might equally well be called Brass. Overemphasis had always been a threat in the eyes of educators who often echoed the sentiments of Cornell's president Andrew White. In 1883 that worthy vetoed a proposed Cornell-Michigan game in Cleveland with the immortal line, "I shall not permit thirty men to travel four hundred miles merely to agitate a bag of wind." Excessive violence was also a threat, with frightening casualty lists of dead and wounded. When Theodore Roosevelt saw a picture of Swarthmore's battered Bob Maxwell after a 1905 game against Penn, he threatened to ban the sport by presidential edict unless rules of order were imposed and enforced. But it was neither the violence nor the significance placed on the game that corrupted it; it was the professionalism born of two kinds of transvaluations.

One is the shifting of emphasis from playing to winning. And when we talk about winning at all costs, we mean both that satisfactory ends justify all means and also that any desired end can be bought at a price. The other concerns the system of organization, the bureaucracy, the power structure, devised to operate, legislate, and facilitate the game. The transvaluation shifts primary motivation to the protection of the system rather than implementation of the system's purposes.

Thus we get professionalism in playing the game and professionalism in managing the game. The result includes such symptoms as the buying of players, the proliferation of coaching staffs, the creation of para-athletic offices of sports promotion and sports information, and the development of organized ways to provide for enriched recruitment budgets and grant-in-aid funds. The latter amounts to a buying of fans to make the buying of players easier. Boosterism begets nothing but its own perpetuity.

When such institutions as the University of Chicago, which had produced distinguished football teams over four decades under Amos Alonzo Stagg, withdrew from intercollegiate competition, many called it idealism. In truth it was the opposite. The idealist would carry on with organized sport, hoping against the evidence to achieve *mens sana in corpore sano* and the integrated, whole self in the pursuit of excellence. But President Hutchins was a realist, a practical man as befitted the head of the institution that had brought John Dewey to Chicago from Ann Arbor in an early demonstration of the academic marketplace. He saw that in practice the ideal was unattainable, and he could not conform to the cynical blinking that marked the attitude of most college administrators toward sports programs.

For the majority of American colleges and universities today, the idealism and the cynicism work together in the practice of the profession, the industry, of intercollegiate athletics. To examine that practice and its values, I propose as a model the University of Maryland and as its spokesman James Kehoe, director of athletics. Kehoe is a Maryland graduate who distinguished himself in World War II. He rose through the ranks to retire as lieutenant colonel, served in the Pacific and Philippines, won four service medals and the bronze star. Before he took over as athletic director, he was the track coach for twenty-three years, during which time he compiled a very distinguished record, culminated in his last year by a great upset IC4A victory over a mighty Villanova team. In the years since he's been athletic director he has led Maryland into national recognition not only in major sports but in a number of so-called minor sports as well.

When Coach Kehoe visited my classroom he welcomed the opportunity to state his positions candidly and fully, instead of being quoted out of context and caricatured by the campus newspapers. Yet instead of sitting with me on chairs in the front of the lecture hall, as all my other guests do, he spent the entire 75 minutes on his feet, marching up and down between me and the class, talking about the American way as he displayed the ever-present flag in his lapel, in what I have come to call his General Patton imitation. He no doubt regarded the session as an adversary proceeding, but I have known him to express the same positions just as forcefully while sitting congenially across the table over a light lunch.

In some ways Kehoe is atypical. His brush cut and loud clothes suggest a throwback to the outback in an age of styled hair and doubleknits or denims. More significant is his unusual commitment to nonrevenue-producing sports—Maryland teams compete with distinction in fencing, wrestling, track, tennis, golf, lacrosse, and swimming—and to intramural sports—he served twenty-five years as intramural director. Most unusual, his program is solvent while over 90 percent of all college programs operate at a deficit. But in terms of philosophy, Kehoe speaks out loud and clear for the athletic establishment.

I would say that there are six major planks in the Kehoe platform. One is the importance of sports; a second is discipline; a third is fiscal integrity; the other three are winning, winning, and winning.

About the role of athletics: it "plays a very positive part or has a very positive place in the total educational picture." This is the traditional idealist position and it is interesting to note that when he expands on this point he talks primarily in terms of participation on every level, developing the values of physical fitness, sportsmanship, teamwork, discipline. "I think you learn that you get out of life just what you put into it—no more and no less. Because I don't care how badly you might want something, if you're not prepared to pay the price and work for it, you're not going to achieve it. And I think the matter of subordinating your own desires at some time to a team effort is important."

On discipline:

let me tell you how Coach Kehoe sees it. I believe totally in discipline. I believe totally in authority. I am a person that believes that, for example, sleep has a whole lot to do with athletics. I am a person that believes that conduct and how you behave youself has a whole lot to do with athletics. But there is a more important thing than this as far as I'm concerned. I believe very strongly that all people must have discipline.

Discipline is something that has to do with watching your weight, getting up and going to class, making yourself study, making yourself be where you're supposed to be when, making yourself assume and accept responsibility and do things that you might not want or like to do. And it's awful easy to do what you like to do but it's difficult to do that which you do not like to do. And I can assure you all that as you live through this life you'll do more things that you don't want or like to do than you will do the things you want to do. I believe appearance, for example, is extremely important. I believe that the young men that visit other institutions and campuses represent Maryland, they represent you and me, and I think that it is important that Maryland be represented well both on and off the court. I believe and I think there is nothing more attractive in life than a well-dressed, well-groomed young lady. Regardless of whether you share this or not, I feel this way about it. It is an asset; it's a plus. It relates to discipline. We do have a curfew because I know that in the athletic world it is important that an athlete get rest if he's going to have to play sixty minutes of football or basketball. I do believe in a study hall because we are very concerned that a student athlete remain eligible and graduate, and I see nothing wrong with this. I totally support being to practice on time.

I totally support rules and regulations in the sense that it is part of a much larger, a much more important and a bigger question. Now it is true that some coaches have different standards of appearance. Frankly, I support the coach. And any coach that isn't consistent with a reasonable I think position is going to find himself in trouble. But I support this because I think it's part of a much larger issue or problem. Now in the climate of the athletic world my remarks are understood and are accepted. I am well aware that in the climate of this particular group I will have great resistance, but still you asked me the question. It is only fair that you should have an honest answer.

The "particular group" he was talking about was a class of 140 students representing a very broad cross-section of the undergraduate community. The dichotomy between the "athletic world" and the academy comes through very impressively, along with the traditionally authoritarian, regimenting, restrictive—if not repressive—attitude of an athletic coach in the academy.

As a "realist," Coach Kehoe sees winning and fiscal integrity as inseparable. I asked if he was proud of his success as director of one of the very few major athletic programs in the country that are commercially sound. He answered, in part,

> Well I think in all both fairness and honesty I would say that I am pleased with it. I don't know about being proud. It is a fact that over ninety percent of intercollegiate athletic departments in this country are in the red. Ours is not. We're having a tough struggle to maintain solvency and to keep our head above water. [Here he discussed rising costs, higher budget, and the diminishing burden carried by the mandatory student athletic fee.] Consequently, the problem or the difficulty of maintaining a fiscally responsible operation has increased and I believe that you shouldn't buy anything unless you can pay for it. I don't believe in operating anything at a deficit. I think this is poor business and I think this is poor philosophy, and I don't support it, and we are making every possible effort through what we believe to be good management and prudent spending of funds and fiscal responsibility, if you please, to see to it that it stays in the black.
>
> I'd be very honest to say, though, that I'm concerned, I'm very apprehensive about the future. I know of no area of business concern or commitment that isn't in trouble. . . . For example, we'd like to maintain the present level of income in basketball, but we're having some difficulty doing it because costs have risen one hundred percent in the last two years. So this is the dilemma.
>
> . . .
>
> In order to survive it becomes more and more important that we do field good teams because I'm sure you all realize that for most people the yardstick in the role of athletics is performance. At Maryland, in particular, we are unique in that I don't know of hardly anywhere else in the country where the competition for the

entertainment dollar is as great as it is here. We've got the Red-skins, we've got the Colts, we've got the Bullets, we've got pro soc-cer, we've got box lacrosse, we've got tennis and a race track on every corner and what have you.

Because we are put in this position it is essential, I think it's al-most self-evident, that for us to be successful, we're going to have to have a good product—I tell you I haven't met many people in life in any area of commitment that they're interested in seeing them lose. And I don't buy losing. That gets you in trouble too. I see nothing commendable or outstanding necessarily about finishing anything but first. First sure beats finishing second. And I want to try and elaborate upon this because I think there are two things here we ought to understand. One I just told you that the realities of life are such, and I'm a realist, if you have a sorry football team or a sorry basketball team, you are not going to support them, the alumni are not going to support them, the students are not going to support them, because this is a matter of record here at Maryland.

Also I believe in winning because, and I want you to hear this very carefully because this is very fundamental and basic to me, I have known winners in my life, and winners, and some of them sit-ting right here, are people that work harder, are better organized, have a greater commitment, a greater dedication, and will pay the price. And I happen to think that's what it's all about. So I view this thing two ways. I know it'll get you an argument, but I don't care if you're an artist, I don't care if you're a musician, I don't care if you aspire to be a publisher, I don't care what you plan or want to be. Whoever you might be in this room, if you don't want to be the best, then you're never going to work for me.

I attempted to pursue these issues in our dialogue. I urged my concern, as a professor in the division of arts and humanities, in hearing so much about profit and loss, about business, and having those kinds of standards influencing in an important way the values of the young people who are students on the univer-sity campus. I said that I understood his concern as a business-man, running an athletic program as a business operation, but I wondered about its significance in carrying over to the thinking of the young people we're trying to educate. His response was that there were valuable lessons in this for the real world after college, for the realities of life.

But isn't there a danger, I asked, in teaching people that there is a monetary value that you can put on everything, including people? Kehoe acknowledged that there were some problems in the recruiting practices, but he wanted Maryland to operate on equal terms with everyone else:

> I'll tell you, if you don't think that many of these institutions aren't actively and aggressively recruiting outstanding you name it or whatever it is, they are. And I see nothing wrong with this. I think this is the American way and I think it's as it should be.
>
> Now I do feel there are certain abuses in recruiting. I think the major area of concern we have in intercollegiate athletics is recruiting. I do believe that in recruiting there has been in many cases such an intense conflict, such intense priority given to this thing that it has been put out of perspective, and I would agree with you there and I support legislation which is now before the national body which would reduce some of these pressures and tensions.

He would neither back away from his position regarding success nor examine the implications of that position to a set of values appropriate to the university:

> I make no bones about it. If this gentleman here wants to be a doctor or a lawyer or an Indian chief, I say that as his or her goal, she should or he should want to be the best. I'll put it to you this way. I never ran a race in my life that I didn't run it to win. I know John Lucas never played, or Mo Howard or anybody else in here, a ball game that they didn't play to win. If I didn't win it, I couldn't wait till the next day to get up and start a little earlier and work a little later and put a little more into it. And I think that is true of your grades, I think that should be true of your goal in life, whatever or whoever you may be or what you want to be.
>
>     . . .
>
> I believe in winning because, I repeat, the people that win are the people that work the hardest and have the greatest commitment and put the most into it. Take Randy White, he was number two

draft choice because he worked for it and he earned it. The same way as these other young men here who I see in the audience, many of whom were just drafted by the NFL. . . . This is the American way. I support it totally. I believe in it one hundred percent and I apply to you, everyone and anyone, I don't care what you want to be in life, you should aim high, you should have a great commitment, and you should aspire to be the *best*.

There are, I take it, many contradictions inherent in the Kehoe position, not the least of which is his insistence on having things two ways at once. He wants to have a university commitment to the appropriateness of athletics in education (I am with him here) so that a mandatory athletic fee for all students is justified (I can't buy this, especially for graduate students). In this he makes a leap from the virtues of participation in sports to the virtues of maintaining intercollegiate competition for the chosen few. But at the same time he wants to have his department operate autonomously as a commercial enterprise, and I find this directly opposite to any reasonable basis for the original commitment.

But let's set aside the philosophical, even the logical, difficulties in Kehoe's stance and entertain some practical considerations—some of the by-products and effects. By his standards, four of the most successful members of the university's staff are part of his own team—Colonel Tom Fields, Russ Potts, Coach Charles G. ("Lefty") Driesell, and Coach Jerry Claiborne. Maryland's athletic program is a profitable one substantially due to Colonel Fields's efforts. An All-American in cross country at Maryland in 1940, he now heads the Maryland Education Foundation, which raises the money from independent sources to fund most of the tuition and other costs for scholarship athletes. His successful fund-raising for 1976 smashed existing records by going over half a million dollars.

Fields is paid by the athletic department at an average full professor's salary. But by a private arrangement with the Foun-

dation he also retains a commission on what he raises. His excellent performance of his salaried job earns him bonuses that
make his income reputedly higher than that of the highest-paid
employee of the university, perhaps of the state, not even count-
ing his Marine Corps pension. Colonel Fields subscribes to the
image of coaches as authoritarians, saying, "If you're going to
produce winning teams and you want to be part of that team you
must adhere to the coach's rules." And again, "It's not run by
committee. The head coach runs it. You don't take a vote.
There's no other way. But there's a way out. If a lad doesn't want
to participate in that, he leaves."

Fields says he believes in the educational program, as befits
the title of his organization: "You're not going to get good athletes
here if you don't give them great academic excellence." But I
think his view of what the university is all about is made clear in
his notion of why people, half of whom are not alumni, contribute
to the Maryland Education Foundation: "They want to be a part
of the program. They like to identify with winners. They've become a real part of the university, of the athletic program." The
athletic program *is* the university in the syntactical construction
of that sentence. Many of these people have nothing to do with
anything else in the university. But some, brought initially to the
campus by sporting events, become involved in other aspects of
the program. Thus a winning record for intercollegiate teams
becomes important for fund-raising in areas other than athletic.
Incidentally, this "real part of the university" is rewarded for its
membership by preferred parking at football and basketball
games, by the privilege to buy tickets for the ACC basketball
tournament, by first preference for tickets to any postseason football and basketball games, and by the privilege of associating
with coaches and players socially in a way that I consider inappro-
priate and artificial.

Tom Fields' exuberant, ruddy, hail-fellow-well-met manner
is ingratiating with Rotary and Kiwanis groups and the like all
across the state. There is no question that he is very good at what

he does. And I am personally indebted to him for finding tickets for me for the 1975 ACC tournament in Greensboro when no one else could and I had no press credentials. But I find it appalling to suppose that his values are assumed by a large percentage of those with whom he deals to be precisely those of the university. Russ Potts, the director of sports promotion, is also given great credit by Kehoe for the program's success. Potts has made Maryland sports into a viable commodity for the advertising dollar in local and even national media. He has also creatively pioneered the commercial tie-in in the selling of college sports to the public. He, too, is salaried by the athletic department, and he is reported to receive additional income in commissions, although I do not know that this is true. It is clear, however, that he has a number of accommodations for sporting events, including press box seats, available for his disposal to or for his business and advertising connections. Recently he turned down an offer to become athletic director at Tulane University; though the base salary was higher, presumably the total income was not.

The idea of creating special promotions to ballyhoo collegiate sports may not be harmful per se. In a sense, pep rallies and competition for symbolic trophies like the Old Oaken Bucket do the same. But when sports promotions become a purely commercial enterprise, that idea has been corrupted. During the 1976 basketball season, Potts repreatedly promoted at Cole Field House a book on Maryland football. Yet my recently published *All the Moves: A History of College Basketball* received not a single mention, even when the Maryland Book Exchange asked that he help to promote an autograph party at the store.

Perhaps more to the point are the following curiosities. I suggested once that Mack Posnak, a basketball Hall-of-Famer who had lived in the Maryland area for many years but was about to retire to Florida, be invited to a game and be introduced to the crowd. Suggestion ignored. After all, a seat for Posnak would bring no new advertiser into the fold. Yet a seat was found for the peripatetic Dancing Harry so that he could do his excruciatingly limited number during a televised game. When Honey Russell, another basketball Hall-of-Famer, died, I suggested that some mention at the next basketball game would be appropriate in deference to Honey's son who is a member of our faculty. Suggestion ignored. After all, a touch of class in public address spots never sold another ticket; in the promotion game, media time is money; and such an announcement had nothing to sell at all. I submit that the very idea of a sports promotion man being considered as a director of athletics is a clear sign of a corruption of values and the subversion of the system.

Coaches Driesell and Claiborne are the most conspicuous of Coach Kehoe's winners. The basketball and football programs under their stewardship have been restored from persistent losers to consistent winners with national rankings. Both have followed an embarrassing pattern of building up win-loss percentages against poor competition, promoting high rankings through media coverage, and then disappointing expectations in big games and postseason play. Both have had spectacular success in recruiting blue-chip prospects, and both have been widely faulted for failing to use their material to full advantage. But both have made their teams into financial successes, doing well at the gate and attracting lucrative media exposure as well.

The achievement of excellence may have escaped them in terms of the highest competition, or of an abstract or aesthetic evaluation of their teams' performances, or of the fulfillment of the team potential of their squads of talented individuals. Yet their achievements are successful by the standards of win-loss ratio and profit-loss marketing. And their personal success has gone far beyond their salaries as relatively highly paid members of the university's payroll community. Their commercial endorsements, their media opportunities, and especially the summer camps they operate with the use of university facilities, all contibute to personal incomes far beyond their salaries or those of any nonathletic-department employee of the university.

Give them credit for their achievements. And don't suppose

for a minute that they don't earn what they get. It is a tribute to Coach Kehoe's team and his leadership that Fields, Potts, Driesell, and Claiborne are among the hardest-working single-directed men in the community. What I am questioning is the value system by which their efforts are measured as successes, which in turn beget additional fruits for their labors, which plums add to the measure of success. It is a chain of self-fulfilling profits, a swallowing of the golden goose that leads to a begetting of a gaggle of golden goslings.

From this mind set, the weak link in Kehoe's team is Jack Zane, the sports information director. He has nothing to sell but reputation, nothing to deal with but empty awards and words. A percentage of the All-American selections from the University of Maryland would earn Jack Zane a commission of newsprint. Yet his success, by any standard other than financial, has been very impressive: an Outland Trophy, All-Americans in several sports, high draft selections, a Rhodes Scholarship. Of course, as Jack is quick to point out, the individuals involved earned their awards; but the fact is that they would not have achieved them in anonymity, without the SID making them celebrities.

Zane displays no displeasure with the ironies of his situation, and he works as hard as his teammates; but sometimes he acts as if the inequities are getting to him—by exercising his power with regard to implementing his notions of a hierarchy among media people, scouts, lackeys, and assorted hangers-on. I am personally indebted to Jack for his many favors to me in my college basketball researches, but occasionally I have been chagrined at what I felt was an unnecessary display of power.

The point I want to make about him is this: even though he does not directly participate in the marketplace mentality that pervades the program, his own performance is indirectly affected by it. He generates extensive press coverage for Steve Sheppard, a Maryland basketball player on the Olympic squad, and virtually neglects Howard Labow, a Maryland foilsman, who at first seemed to have a much better chance of making the trip to Montreal until a pre-Games tournament occasioned an injury that kept him out of action for the American fencing team. The D.C. area papers did not report that Labow had made the squad nor that he was subsequently hurt. Zane plays up every possible angle about football and basketball, even during off-seasons, while the lacrosse team—for several years Maryland's finest athletic competitor—languishes in relative obscurity even in the state where interest in that sport is greatest.

No wonder he is "very positive" about colleges supplying professional football and basketball with cost-free minor leagues. "Every person should have the opportunity to prepare for his chosen profession," he has said, in what seems like a proper principle for a public institution. But it really reflects a trade-school notion of higher education that itself is based on a monetary value system, an ends-justify-means ethic, a quantification of all values.

His greatest satisfaction must have come from the success of John Lucas. The first man chosen in the 1976 NBA draft, Lucas had already agreed to contract terms with Houston before the drafting began. And then within a couple of weeks he had also signed a professional tennis contract with the Golden Gaters of World Team Tennis. In the specialized, professionalized world of intercollegiate athletics, a two-sport All-American is the rarest of birds. Lucas's success, measured in terms of the dollars on his contracts, is the best tribute to Kehoe's program and the best copy Jack Zane could distribute. The dollars are not directly shared by Kehoe or Zane (or by Lucas's coaches, Driesell and Doyle Royal), but they are the signs of success for them all.

Those lucrative professional contracts for Randy White, Len Elmore, and Tom McMillen pay off in another way—their value in recruiting. Recruitment is at the heart if not the root of all the evils in collegiate athletics. Recruiting practices (and their attendant and I think inevitable corruptions) are the result of pernicious transvaluations I have been talking about, and they nourish and refuel those very values that produce them. By centering part of the ensuing discussion around recruitment, then, we can examine the effects of what I have labeled the Kehoe position on athletes and athletics, on students in general and on the process of education.

But I do not want to appear to be setting up James Kehoe as a straw man or as the devil incarnate. He is far from being an extreme case. He does not suffer from either of the two characteristic ills of his profession—the football mentality by which, at the most, two sports get all attention and budget; and the image-conscious slipperiness by which authoritarianism is masked and the whole operation is glazed over with a bright haziness that effectively screens the light of day or public scrutiny. Kehoe is forthright and forthcoming in most regards, and he is a staunch supporter of nonrevenue-producing sports, seeking and demanding the pursuit of excellence everywhere in the program. Yet the philosophy that guides him and the application of the principles under which he operates have bred a frightening phantasmagoria of transvaluations.

The athletes have a word for the special treatment they receive that sets them apart from all other students—"handled." But it is not often understood that some of them are handled more and better than others, according to rather arbitrary perceptions of potential, performance, and cooperativeness. It all begins with recruiting. Kim Hoover, a wide receiver at Maryland who received a contract from the Baltimore Colts but is attending law school, said that he "looked forward to the excitement of travel and being taken to this and that. When it came, it turned out to be a pain." But Hoover is unusual, a Phi Beta Kappa history major who openly criticized his coach's play selections. He was a golden boy, a high school blue chipper, and in much demand.

More typical is the case of a lineman who happened to be noticed in a film. A recruiter called to say he was being considered a prospect. As he described it in his journal for my course, "Then came my brush with big time recruiting. They brought me to the campus, took me to dinner, sent me to a basketball game, and sent me home in the morning. Where were the loose girls and easy money? Hell, I didn't even meet the head coach." A week later he was offered a scholarship and eventually accepted it, with some misgivings about his chances for successfully doing college work.

There was a problem about his admission. His average and class ranking were low so that he had to score well on the College Boards. He tried once and "didn't come close." Then, "some people associated with the University on a volunteer basis offered to help me find someone to take the Boards for me. I declined and said I would take care of it myself. They said to let them know what it costs me, and that they would reimburse me for it. I got it done for nothing by a friend and pocketed $30 from the Maryland people. I needed the money for my high school prom."

This player went on to talk about popular misconceptions about the free ride of the college jock. "We are not all superheroes, superstuds, loaded with free gifts and money. I spent five years here, started for three varsity seasons and became relatively well known to Maryland sports enthusiasts." That thirty dollars he pocketed for his prom was the only time he was ever handled. Yet he believes that his experience is rare, that many players are handled often. Without bitterness he says that people should not automatically assume that all athletes are corrupted, though many are.

I expected to find that there was a feeling among the young athletes during the recruiting process that they were being exploited, treated as a commodity in a kind of high-class slave market. But this does not appear to be so. Apparently they are already cynical or sophisticated enough to know what to expect and to get theirs in the system. For a Kim Hoover, he didn't feel it because, as he says, "I didn't need it." If he wanted to go to an Ivy League school, his parents would have sent him, so he was making his choice on his own terms. For a John Lucas, he felt it only in the sense that people would try to impress him with a soul-brother handshake to make him think they were hip to or sympatico with blacks. But that they were embracing a value system in which they were being used as items of commercial currency does not come consciously through to them at the time.

What does come through very quickly is the perception of their role with relation to a head coach. In my experience, athletes unanimously accept the notion that authoritarian coaches are egomaniacs. One basketball player pointed to his coach's manner of dress and public behavior as signs of egomania, suggesting that he celebrates his birthday on Christmas. Football players at Maryland talk about being "under contract to Jerry D. Claiborne." Tom Scarbath, whose father was an All-American quarterback at Maryland and is now on the Board of Regents, put it this way in his journal:

> When you sign an athletic grant-in-aid you are not only subjecting yourself to the "guidance" of the NCAA and its regulations but also to any rules or whims that your head coach wishes to enact. Curfews, dress codes, hair and conduct codes are only the more superficial ones. In order to play football here at Maryland you must compromise any attitudes that conflict with Claiborne's or at least appear to be doing so in order to play for him. Of course it all depends on your ability; i.e., players of vast ability are sometimes excused from regulations.

Hoover talked about resenting curfew; as a serious student, it put him at a disadvantage in competing in the classroom with students who had many more hours to read. Lucas listed a number of items for resentment: curfew, the clean-shaven rule, the "monkey-suits" for travel, study hall. It's very hard to put up with, he said, "unless you know how to slip out and slip in." But they do put up with it, and both Hoover and Lucas said it was definitely worth it. They both contributed greatly to a commercially successful operation, but both are satisfied with what they personally derived from the association. Again, these two exceptional men may not accurately reflect the typical experience of college athletes with respect to their sports and what they get from their "contracts."

Another view comes from the journal of Alan Bloomingdale, starting fullback on the 1974 team, now a stock broker after two years of pro football in the NFL and CFL:

> I am attending this university on an athletic scholarship. I participate under the auspices of Jerry D. Claiborne. But *I play* for Alan D. Bloomingdale. This attitude caused much unrest within the framework of Cole Field House and the offices therein.
>
> My teammates called me a free spirit, the press called me a nonconformist, Claiborne called me a problem. I just thought I should be Alan and nothing more. I quickly learned that the individual is not tolerated in this system of football.
>
> I noticed that I was a favorite with the reporters after games. I knew I was no hero, and what I did on the field did not attract that kind of attention, but I learned that they would always talk to me because I would speak the truth. Many times throughout the season my mouth got me in a lot of trouble. I was told what I could say and what I couldn't say, no matter what the truth might be. But I thought Alan should act like Alan and not be a puppet. After one article in the *Star* by Dick Heller, I was told, "Alan, if I had a fullback that could even do a halfway decent job, I would set your butt on the bench." There were many statements of that nature uttered in my direction, but that is the one I like.
>
> Football used to be fun, but college has changed my mind about that. This university has stripped any love for football I ever had. So you ask me why I am going to the New England Patriots next year. So I ask you, what else can I do? My whole life has been football. I guess I hope I can find that love I once had for football. I hope, I pray, that I can grow to love the game the way I did before I came here and met Jerry D. Claiborne. I am not bitter. I am just thankful it is over.

Here, too, the perception of subordinating self to coach comes through. But an even stronger perception grows with it—the distinctions among the star players, the regulars, and the substitutes. The system seems to impose a caste structure, and presumably this is useful to the coaches. At the University of South Carolina, for example, Paul Dietzel compounded the ghettoizing of athletes by having a special house for starters, and he moved players in and out during the season as their performances and ranking dictated.

I asked Hoover and Lucas, who were so positive about the program, what's wrong with it, if anything? Hoover objected to the fact that it was "too success-oriented." He talked about the pressures of representing your family, your school, your home-town, etc., but not your *self*, and said, "You are rated as a person by how you perform as a player." Lucas said simply, "Only the top players get the rewards."

Tom Scarbath's journal explored this point a little more:

> Sports today, with very few exceptions, are only lucrative to the first stringers and superstars. In college *all but* the first one and a half teams are used to run the opposing team's plays and more often than not are actually used as dummies themselves. Speaking only from my experience here, third and fourth teamers are made to take great risks to their bodies in order "to give a good picture" to the starters. And then, if a team is losing the non-starters have the starters' frustrations vented on them in preparation for the next game.

John Schultz, Maryland's sterling wingback, blocker, short-yardage-gainer, first-down-receiver, and kick-returner, now with the Denver Broncos, probably put it best of all: "Some believe that coaches like to take on the father image. What I would ask is, who fathers the third and fourth teams?"

The degree to which players must conform to coaches' ideas clearly relates to how important they are to coaches' plans. The following story is taken from a player's journal, and I have substi-tuted X for his teammate's name:

> X was an individual, not a trouble-maker, an A student. From February through April we have workouts four times a week. Now the NCAA says that it is illegal to have mandatory workouts during

this time because they feel these months should be given to the student to catch up on academics. Our coach gets by on this point by making it a class offered by the University and calling it a voluntary practice. What the NCAA doesn't know is that all the regular students that sign up for this class are put in a separate group from the regular football players. Also, the ballplayers are told they cannot miss a practice or they will be run on the week ends (what happened to voluntary?). Then they proceed to make practices so hard the students quit. They are usually gone after the first week. Then things get tough.

Well, X was missing practice here and there. When he was asked why, he told them he was trying to catch up on work and also attending tutoring sessions and taking tests. X is a pre-med student (something the coaching staff frowns upon). He was told not to miss another practice or he would be in trouble.

X pointed out that the practices were not supposed to be mandatory. He was quickly told that if he missed practice his scholarship would be taken away. He missed practice again a few days later. When asked why, he said he took a test. He was told that was too bad and they told him to go home.

X then went to Kehoe and explained that if his scholarship was taken away he would tell the NCAA what was going on. They put him back on scholarship. When spring ball started he was put on the last team and was used like a dummy. After each practice the coaches would keep X out for "special" help. They would run him and make him do grass drills till he fell down. Then they would walk off and leave him. They didn't quit.

If it had been me they were abusing I would have left, but not X. He made it, the whole spring—every day.

The summer went by and we reported this year for training camp. X came back—the coaches went nuts. They told him to leave. He said no. So after a few days of practice and a few "help" sessions for X, Coach Claiborne kicked X off. Why? He told the team that X was overweight.

X is a good guy and the team loves him. He beat Mr. Claiborne and everybody knew it. Jerry couldn't stand to see someone he couldn't control—so he removed him. That's what he does to everything he can't control—he removes it.

What happened to sportsmanship and fair play?

This is not, I suppose, an uncommon story. And it is not in the same league with horror stories like the familiar one about two players being shut into a room and told by the coach, "The one who walks out of here will get the starting job." Yet the story of X scores several points about the erosion of values.

In the coaches' caste system, the lowest order of being is the walk-on. The following story is paraphrased, except where quoted verbatim, from the journal of Bill Deoudes, who almost made the Maryland football team as a walk-on. It is a story of physical brutality taken as a matter of course, but it is, I think, a psychological and ethical horror story.

> On September 7, 1974, in the intra-squad Red-White game a week before the opener with Alabama, I was the White punter, Phil Waganheim the Red. "My first few punts proved disastrous. On my first punt a violent rush, featuring Randy White and company vs. the freshmen who were blocking for me, but I managed to get that one off for 41 yards." On the second punt the ball was tipped by, I think, Harry Walters and went out of bounds while he, Jim Santa, Randy White, and others ended up on top of me—no roughing because of the partial block. On the third punt, I think it was Vince Kinney who plowed into me; he missed the ball but no roughing was called. On the fourth punt, "Randy White came through the line untouched and wiped out the ball and me. After all, if you were a freshman and had to block Randy White, would you?"
>
> As the second half started I wondered why a dummy wasn't being used instead of me so that the first team defense could practice their punt rush against an inexperienced freshman line. Phil, punting for the Red team, hadn't even been threatened no less touched. But I went dumbly on and when I punted again the following seven things happened:
>
> 1. They put on a ferocious ten-man rush.
> 2. The snap was in the dirt to my right and I lost time retrieving it.
> 3. Ernie Salley and Vince Kinney collided in mid-air, changing the direction of their rush so that they both hit my right knee. (I got the punt off, so a roughing penalty was called.)

4. My right medial-collateral ligament was torn "to strands and shreds."
5. My "anterior-cruciary ligament was torn completely off the bone."
6. The inside cartilege was also torn and had to be removed.
7. "Any dreams of playing organized football again were just about ended for me."

I lay in the hospital for five days, my leg swollen "in plaster from my toes to my ass. Coach Claiborne came to see me and told me it was a stupid thing to happen and that I should work on it and get ready for spring ball." I really believed he was concerned, but it occurred to me later that he was probably thinking, "Well at least Randy and Louis [Carter] performed well."

I worked hard on the knee every chance I had and "when spring came around I went out and began to perform. Through five weeks of practice I got progressively better each day. Three days before the spring Red-White game I found out I wasn't to suit up, that Sochko would punt for both squads."

I asked Coach Claiborne what happened and he said that I wasn't "ready to be put under fire" because they were afraid the leg wasn't strong enough yet. He said my status was "injured player." I questioned this because injured players sit inside and don't practice with the team, but I had practiced for five weeks. Well, he said, "To tell you the truth Mike Sochko is going to be kicking for us in the fall."

The message he was really trying to send was this: "Bill, we didn't recruit you, you walked on. If you were to make it, now that we're big time, it would make our recruiting staff look bad. You're not on scholarship, so you haven't been put under fire because we don't want to pay for another one of *your* operations."

Deoudes concludes that Claiborne is, like many other college coaches, an egomaniac who doesn't care what he has to do as long as he looks good. But at no time does he really acknowledge the value system that coaches embrace and players accept. Perhaps it takes a great sophistication or cynicism to say, as John Lucas has said, "Hell, it *is* professional. The coach's *job* is on the line. Why *shouldn't* he put failures on the players?" And why should the players accept the system? Presumably, for them, the rewards are great enough. They have been trained and conditioned, as indeed our whole society has, to believe that athletes are a special breed and deserve to be handled.

Doug Radebaugh, an All-American midfielder in lacrosse when he was at Maryland, talked about this in a discussion of *Rabbit, Run,* where he traces Harry Angstrom's problems to this conditioning, including his problems with women:

> What type of women do athletes prefer or with which type do they find the most satisfying relationships? First of all, probably because of his own interest in physical fitness and "the body beautiful," the athlete wants an attractive and well-built girl. A good-looking lady is needed to complement the athlete. Then I think there is a strong emphasis on the sexual relationship. The athlete is a physically oriented person who wants to exert his body in many ways; he cannot, in most cases, find happiness from much mental stimulation.
>
> This also leads to another point: the athlete requires and often demands a lot more attention than many people. [They] get special treatment and feel they deserve special attention. They demand this from their women, possibly asking often for too much, but for the most part I think the women look to these men as their idols and thus must take care of their "babies" to keep things OK. When out on the town many athletes have the attitude that they're God's gift to women, but then again many women eat it up being with a "star." Many women thrive on fulfilling his every need.
>
> [These attitudes are cultivated by the special treatment athletes often get from their parents.] Not all athletes are self-centered, spoiled egotists, but many do seem to feel they are just a bit extra special. I think many athletes forget how many athletes have come before them and will follow. If an athlete realized how quickly he'd be forgotten he might not thrive on the thoughts of himself as a superstar, but then again how are you going to convince an athlete he's just one of many when he hears the roar of the crowd on the day of the game.

The rewards are not all measurable in quantities of statistics and dollars, then. There is still the sheer joy of performance and the adulation of the crowd. But it might be argued, too, that striving for these rewards is not altogether compatible with the kind of striving that should go into a college education. This point was made very well in a journal entry by a hard-working basketball substitute who tried to explain why he missed his classes on the first day of the semester. There happened to be an important game that night, and that was all that mattered. In retrospect, the game (his team won; he didn't play) seemed less important, and he felt some guilt and self-contempt for confusing his priorities. He concluded with an analogy of sports to drugs—a rush of self-importance and power followed by a sudden return to reality with depression and self-loathing that ultimately requires another fix.

From these introspective perceptions, I anticipated subsequent examinations of sports in this journal from the vantage point of an active player, albeit a substitute, who would come to question an absolute quantification of values. It did not happen, perhaps because he didn't work at it, perhaps because I didn't get through to him, but probably because the system and its ways of subverting other values are too deeply hidden and cleverly masked in the jockocracy.

John Lucas might have been expected to respect and pursue academic values. His mother was his junior high school principal, his father his high school principal. "I studied real hard for the first six weeks," he said, "and didn't do well at all on my first exams. Then I decided to do as most of my peers do, and then I started to do better." The peers he mentions are fellow athletes who know ways of getting handled academically, who handle each other, and who are advised by coaches to cultivate any form of handling that will keep them eligible. (Do you suppose they are aware of the homosexual and masturbatory implications of their diction?) That the handling may also keep them from getting the education that is the ostensible purpose of the scholarship means nothing to the athletic department.

Even the virtue of a variety of social contact is denied to the athlete. He is separated in his living arrangements and his life style. Lucas says that Coach Driesell wanted to have a fraternity-type house for the basketball team in 1975–76, but the players objected because they wanted the "college life of the dorm." Maryland has no exclusive athletic dorm (which at first disappointed Lucas who expected maids and carpets), but the teams live together each on a floor of the same high-rise dorm with the football team on the top two floors. Kim Hoover opposes this practice, saying that after four or five years, football players "know a lot of girls, but maybe not more than 15–20 guys outside the team." His recommendation is directly to the point: "Treat athletes like other people."

Maybe that's the problem. Maybe we have allowed athletes to be corrupted by the standards of other people. Or maybe now we are conceiving a society in which all other people are taught to think like contemporary athletes and athletic directors: build up your winning percentage, win at all costs, if the other guy is bending or dodging the rules you better outbend and outdodge him, and whatever you do show a profit. If our colleges are not teaching their athletes anything else, what happens when the athletes teach their colleges this value system? How can educational values be quantified? And how, other than by embracing a totalitarian model of trade preparation, can education be measured in a practical, profit-and-loss way?

I have expert testimony from two more witnesses to call before my closing argument. One is my friend and colleague Jack Russell, a distinguished scholar of modern British fiction and style and satire. His father was the legendary Honey Russell, one of the greatest athletes of the first half of this century. He played pro baseball with Shoeless Joe Jackson, pro football for George Halas, and especially pro basketball, where his famous battles with Nat Holman often saw the Celtic star held to few points or even none. Honey went on to coach Seton Hall, Manhattan College, the Boston Celtics, and Seton Hall again, where he won an NIT championship with the Walter Dukes–Richie Regan team.

Up to his recent death he was still active in sports as a scout for the Chicago White Sox.

Jack sees no conflict now and remembers none in his youth between his academic commitment and his family's athletic involvement. As a boy he was "always thinking about wins and losses," he says, "which made life interesting." He says that to his father semi-pro baseball was as important as pro basketball. Russell's first year with the brand-new Celtics was a bad one, in part, because they were delayed in organizing when he insisted on fulfilling his commitment to the Rutland, Vermont, baseball team.

How did it feel, I asked Jack, to have so much depending on the result of a game? "It made you feel alive," he said, remembering those nights of waiting for his father to call home with a report. "Incidentally, he never said 'we lost' but only 'we got beat.' " Jack also remembers developing juvenile superstitions and behavior patterns, stemming from feelings of responsibility, that what he did somehow influenced the games.

What does that do to your sense of values? I asked, hoping for an insight into corruption and subversion.

"Makes you accept losses, the second-rate, the failure of expectations." He went on to talk about Seton Hall's basketball team in 1953 when two surprising late-season losses preceding the NIT left them 31–2 instead of a record 33–0, and how he is glad now that they fell short of perfection. He then made a useful distinction between prediction and anticipation, the one simply a projection of wish fulfillment and the other a way of making concrete adjustments to the variables of forthcoming experience.

ISAACS: Are sports overemphasized in the university?

RUSSELL: No, because the audience is there. Oh, some coaches tend to overemphasize, they overwork players, overreview opponents, scrutinize films umpteen times instead of just once. And sports are hurt by overlapping, attenuated seasons. This encourages athletes' greed, also entrepreneurs and promoters not intimately associated with sport.

ISAACS: I'm going to throw you a curve ball, because the example is one I heard from your father: A very hot baseball prospect that several big-league clubs were after, bids going up to six-figure bonuses. He was also an outstanding football player, courted by a number of college football coaches. He turned down final baseball offers to accept a deal at a Southeastern Conference football school, and his reason was that in the long run he was going to do better. Are we talking now about the greed of the athlete or are we talking about something entirely different? Aren't we really talking about the fact that there is so much emphasis on buying a winning team that the athlete himself is not showing the greed, he is accepting the monetary value that is put upon him by the other people, the recruiters, the fan clubs, the fans themselves?

RUSSELL: This is a younger player. In this context, the fault lies with the under-the-table four-year arrangement at the college, with its accommodation of all these people. It's damn hard to blame the situation on a seventeen- or eighteen-year-old athlete.

ISAACS: My point is that they're not out for all they can get for themselves, but they learn at this early age that they are a commodity and so the commodity thinking is forced upon them. Very few of them are able ever to get out of that syndrome that has developed with having a commercial, a financial value put on their bodies and their physical abilities.

RUSSELL: It's certainly more that way than it ever was. It wasn't that way when it wasn't possible to become a millionaire. Except for Red Grange and Babe Ruth, it wasn't possible to make such strides, whereas it's possible for dozens or maybe scores of athletes today. And I suppose that sooner or later they are going to realize what a dead end that commodity thinking is. Some are wise enough to keep perspective all along. Many have agents and lawyers and pay people to keep other people away. That used to be true only in the fight game. Fighters used to have agents galore, stables getting rake-offs. Team athletes—never. Now every team athlete has to have a lawyer and at least one agent. This kind of pimping, for example, that the athletes get caught in, it's almost a status symbol to have a stable of agents and lawyers. It's horrendous, and the athletes themselves always get the short end. They don't make their own decisions. Someone else tells them what to do. When they're younger it's their parents who sit down with the scouts, but at least it's people intimately involved with their real life. In this later phase, it's people who are not involved with their real life, only their commodity life—and it's a precious thing. Every athlete sooner or later finds out how treacherous all this is.

ISAACS: As members of a university community that stresses its athletic prominence, aren't we taking part in promulgating this set of values?

RUSSELL: No, not if we don't worry one iota when we lose a Moses Malone. We must accept it with great equanimity, never getting upset by losing a commodity in this great body market.

Reviewing this interview now I realize that I should have picked up the point about getting upset. It seems to me that we should get upset about the recruiting of Moses Malone and, in the same year, Brett Vroman from Provo, Utah—not because Malone turned pro before leading Maryland to the promised land of a national title and not because Vroman chose UCLA and probably never had any intention of coming to College Park, not even because of the unspecified fortune that was spent on these tall prospects, but because of the implications of those losses and expenses; not how much revenue and contributions must be generated to make up for them and replace them in the crop of the next harvest time, but *how* it is generated and *why*. The answers—*anyway at all* and *to do it all over again*—damn well should upset us, as it upsets the structure and mission of the academy. My final witness is a guest I introduced to the class as two people, my friend and colleague John Howard, the Blake scholar, and the legendary Hezzie Howard, the all-time All-American attackman at Washington College who coached lacrosse at Maryland for several years while pursuing a humanistic career in English.

ISAACS: Did you feel schizoid?

HOWARD: That's exactly the feeling I had, but I think it's a cultural thing. The schizophrenia came because the people I knew who were involved in sports were not the people who were involved in humanistic activities, and each group's mores and values were so different that I felt that I was shifting from one name, Hezzie Howard, to another, John Howard, for a while—but after a while I became aware that the same mental capacities were being used in both endeavors. The essence of a coach, as far as I could see, was the capacity to analyze human motions, human relationships. The coach looks at a game and its objectives. He tries to organize his players in such a way as to help them achieve the game's objectives. This requires that he analyze all the things that the players are doing and put them together in a coherent way. When I study literature I also see what the purpose is. It has a goal. I have to decide what the individual parts are that go together to make up the whole. That requires analysis. The so-called schizophrenia is a socially induced rather than naturally separated kind of experience. In the long run the two activities are simply different facets of the same activity of the mind—to analyze a process and put the parts together after analysis.

ISAACS: But the goal is so completely different that . . .

HOWARD: No it isn't.

ISAACS: What's your purpose in analyzing your team in lacrosse?

HOWARD: To win the next game and to win as many games as you can.

ISAACS: How is that analogous with analyzing Blake's poetry?

HOWARD: In essence when I was analyzing a team's structure in order to make it win, I had to ask myself what winning represents. In my case winning represented the results of analysis, when I had my team do something new or different. I had created in order to get some kind of satisfaction, called winning. When I analyze a work of literature I am essentially looking for an understanding, but that understanding is after all a kind of pleasure or satisfaction. In essence I create, in my mind from the material I abstract from the literature, something new. That kind of pleasure I see as not very different from the pleasure of creating a team effort that wins. I get the same kind of thrill in discovering the way a poem that is very difficult goes together and how it has meaning to me as I got out of putting together a successful effort on a lacrosse team.

ISAACS: I can accept that because I've experienced the same kind of identity. There is a relatively similar satisfaction in correctly doping a horse race and figuring out for the first time what a poem means when for a thousand years no one knew what it meant.

How about the assertion that I've made that the values taught in athletics are contrary to the values we're trying to teach in the humanities?

HOWARD: The values inherent in team sports are not only not contradictory to what is being done in humanistic study but they're complementary and almost the same thing. But there is a kind of degeneration in team sports which is caused perhaps by the large financial benefits from having a winning team in the pros or the sense of self-gain that any individual can get out of a team sport. This is a corrupting influence on what is basic in a team sport and the same thing can happen in humanistic study. Rather than genuinely pursuing knowledge a professor can be pursuing a promotion.

But in general the values are the same. Team sports carry out a training process, one of the most fundamental in human nature. Humanistic study carries out another training process that is also fundamental. They are slightly different but both absolutely essential. In a team sport an individual must learn inevitably that his own personal gain, his own personal joy, not only cannot supersede the team but cannot be satisfied unless the team itself is a success. One function of literature is indoctrination into society. As you read about other human experiences you must necessarily empathize with those experiences, subordinate yourself for a moment. While you're reading *The Great Gatsby* you become the Great Gatsby who is not you, who is someone else. You learn what the experience of someone like the Great Gatsby is within a society and you become aware of how it is important that there are certain parts of yourself that cannot be put above society.

So both are forms of training in order to fit into society. If there's any corruption, it's that both forms have been so goddamn successful in our culture that we have too many people fitting too easily into society and as a consequence instead of thinking for themselves accept vague directions from outside themselves.

ISAACS: This suggests that all humanistic study, like all participation in athletics, has a pragmatic end.

HOWARD: Yes, the pragmatic end is the survival of society. Sports evolved, literature evolved, speech and movies evolved, like everything to contribute to the survival of society.

ISAACS: Doesn't humanistic study in our time suggest that society may not survive, that humanistic study may not survive, that in fact humanistic study is not likely to survive, because of the pragmatic factors that have taken over in education? Our university tends more and more to quantify values and therefore the arts and humanities and pure sciences . . .

HOWARD: OK, there are indications of trouble. It's like having a losing team on a court or a field. When you have trouble, you start looking for new methods. But when society is in trouble, instead of thinking people start adding and subtracting. Instead of looking at things qualitatively, they begin to quantify. Yet trouble doesn't predict the end. Sometimes it's a way of bringing forth greater effort, challenging the team to change its patterns of behavior on the field so it will win and challenging the thinking process so it will come out with a better answer. If you don't have problems, you generally don't have very great response. Stagnation is a bigger problem than threats.

ISAACS: Isn't all sport primarily based on a quantification of values and isn't that antithetical to the basis of humanistic study?

HOWARD: You mean that sport is built on scoring which then measures whether you've won or lost? I have an answer that isn't terribly satisfactory: it may be possible to have enough intelligence that you probably could reduce all you know to numerical terms.

ISAACS: Spoken like a former administrator.

HOWARD: No, spoken like a person who believes in physics. The fact is, you don't know enough now to make it work. Computers only work with rather simple things. Computers can't yet quantitize qualities of thought meaningfully. Sport is a rather simplified quantitization, but the process that goes on in achieving this simple thing is a process of training that allows humans to generalize the training into more significant social functions.

ISAACS: We are part of a university that is proud of its athletic record because it shows a profit. At the same time we are being instructed that we have to shift our attention to the profit-making areas of the university and positions have to be transferred from arts and humanities and mathematics over to those areas of the university which are more productive in the same kind of profit-making terms.

HOWARD: First of all, the notion that the big sports, basketball and football, make a profit is one of the reasons I'm not coaching any more. If you took the actual football gate and put it up against the expenses of the football team I doubt very seriously that you'd see a profit. But if you take the total athletic sale which includes the sale of athletic tickets to students—who by the way if they all come couldn't get in to see a football game anyway—then that extra money turns it all into a profit. But it obscures the truth to say that athletics in this university show a profit; it's a profit at the expense of robbing students of their money. On the other hand, when you talk about shifting academic positions around, I have a different kind of response. Money—profit—is an indication of human interest. There are more people interested in sociology now than English. The explanation of human interest has degenerated to the language of profit, so we look at our having to shift positions as a process in a profitable kind of enterprise. The language of banking has invaded the athletic realm where it's simply not stated accurately (I think that's a bunch of hogwash). And the language has invaded the academic marketplace (the very word suggests it), but there is a very real human interest in other academic fields which needs to be met.

ISAACS: The language doesn't induce the values, does it? The values embody the language. We borrow that language because we have been convinced that those values do indeed apply.

HOWARD: You mean that we believe that quantitization, the number of people who want to take sociology, will end up determining our values? I believe in the long run that's probably true. But I don't see that humanistic study in any way goes against that.

ISAACS: In academic terms, can you justify the kind of athletic program that the University of Maryland operates? Is it appropriate for higher education to organize intercollegiate competition?

HOWARD: I've always asked myself that. I never have had a clear answer. Pragmatically it is very useful in a number of ways.

ISAACS: In psychological terms?

HOWARD: In psychological terms and economic terms. I have a naïve faith that a state legislature gives more to a school when a winning football team is there. I think problems that the university has with the state legislature would be much worse if we had a losing football team. Winning is important. Psychologically, winning teams become something we can identify with, and human beings need a sense of high self-esteem. I know that I feel that when the basketball and the football teams win I am involved in the victory and I feel better that I am at Maryland because they're winning teams.

But your real question was, is it academically suitable? People participating in team sports learn something very important in life. In that sense I'd say it's quite significant. The heartache is that not enough people are involved in sports. More people are involved by empathy.

ISAACS: What is it that they learn that is valuable?

HOWARD: The whole process of fitting into a group. When businesses used to send people here on recruiting trips, they would always ask about participating in team sports. It was the best sign of people who knew how to fit in, as opposed to antisocial types. There is a danger, of course, because total subordination to the group leads to a mindless existence; then the group is blindly driven rather than directed by human intelligence. It all goes back to man's need to herd. Sports condition man to subordinate himself to the herd. Men can't survive as individuals.

ISAACS: Is sport then a ritualization of a primitive herd instinct?

HOWARD: Not ritualization, training.

ISAACS: That we don't get in many other ways?

HOWARD: One form of training to fit into the herd.

ISAACS: Then the best kind of training would be the most authoritarian kind of training which would insist on subordinating the individual. It would tend to support the Lombardi kind of coach. Were you the Lombardi kind of coach?

HOWARD: No, I disagree with that. Some sports are better than others for this kind of training. Basketball, lacrosse, hockey require nonverbal communication. You see eyes, hands, body gestures; you have to make instant decisions, immediate responses to situations.

ISAACS: Wouldn't the most rigidly authoritarian coach more successfully predict responses of individuals in given situations?

HOWARD: I've seen the most rigid authoritarian coaches fail horribly. They lacked brains, the capacity to analyze. Failing coaches never learn that, in practice, perfect predictability is impossible. . . . Coaches can help a team only by not hurting them. . . . Coaches working teams up to emotional pitch—hogwash. Overly emotional teams stop playing.

Overcoaching is the worst sin in my book. Thus I do not believe an authoritarian coach is particularly useful.

ISAACS: You're pretty authoritarian about that.

HOWARD: Yes. The extreme is the kind of coach who decides that the players are all going to cut their hair the same way and wear the same clothes. He forgets that the athlete's ability is to throw the ball, to run, to score a goal and not how he fits into the coach's ideas of a social order. Team spirit exists on the field, it exists for the moment, and what the individual does before and after that is usually irrelevant.

ISAACS: How about recruiting? Is it appropriate to an academic environment?

HOWARD: I would never be able to say myself that recruiting good material was antithetical to a good academic environment.

ISAACS: What about aggression in sports?

HOWARD: One of the things that bug me that I read in scientific journals is the notion that sports is a way of expressing aggression. This doesn't make sense to me. In my experience as a player and a coach, I saw sport as an expression of a team spirit and aggression as a by-product of it. In fact you cannot play a sport and be as aggressive as your individual response might suggest. Even in football there are rules. You must try to avoid basically hostile acts, to keep your aggression within certain bounds.

If you were playing a sport simply because it was aggressive you would quickly become very bored with the sport. What you're playing for is the thrill of belonging to a team and the thrill of victory. It's that team feeling which is reinforced, and the aggression is not actually expressed at all. In fact, after a game if you've lost, even though you might have been very active during the game, you'll feel a hell of a lot more aggressive than you felt before; so that the game itself doesn't in any sense express aggression and get rid of it. And there are certain kinds of losers that go around showing aggression all the time. So I don't believe that aggression has a hell of a lot to do with team sports. A sport like boxing or wrestling, maybe so, but I would suggest that even there the skill is at least as important as the expression of aggression.

John Howard's construction supplies the most persuasive rationale for the presence of team sports alongside humanistic study in the colleges. But it is a rationalization for corrupt practices in the name of an ideal that doesn't exist in any Athens of the West any more than it persisted in ancient Greece. In practice, team sports are treated just like individual sports. Competition in tennis, golf, swimming, track, and others is structured and scored according to a team concept which has little to do with the actual play of those sports. On a grand scale this nonsense carries over to the Olympic Games where national "teams" are valued in the media in terms of numbers of medals.

Intercollegiate athletes are bid for and bought in what might perversely be called an open market. They are sold up the river into a ghettoized, sacrosanct precinct in which they are handled—but selectively. The stars can retain a sense of individuality in return for their services. The starters are remunerated in terms of hierarchical status, peer prestige, and the perqs of professionalism. The substitutes do what they're told and they get to stay in the herd, hoping to move up in rank.

In intercollegiate athletics huge coaching and recruiting staffs are necessary to compete with other schools. Winning teams are necessary to justify the staffs. The staffs are necessary to produce the wins. The wins are necessary to sell the tickets and rate TV exposure. The income is necessary to justify the expense of producing the wins. Talk about a vicious cycle, there seems no end to this circular thinking. And there is the old story of the original substantive purposes becoming secondary to the purpose of sustaining the formal machinery and perpetuating the power structure.

In colleges, where the value of participation in sports at every level is honored in theory, the practice is for intercollegiate competition to take precedence at the expense of all other levels. I have often been asked if I support the idea of intercollegiate athletics in the first place. The answer is yes, because I believe that the striving for excellence in sports should be rewarded by a natural process of rising to advanced levels. I conceive of a very simple pyramid structure in which the winners advance (an elimination tournament draw sheet is just a pyramid on its side). But the apex must be supported by the broad base of universal partipation. The way it stands now, the pyramid structure as well as the value system is inverted. Instead of participation we have only surrogate satisfaction. And in one way or another the nonparticipants pay both for the very existence of intercollegiate performances and also for the privilege of watching them.

The values of such a system carry over to the university at large in many ways. Widespread cheating is tacitly accepted as a matter of course. Many feel forced to cheat in order to compete equally with others who do. Departments that produce more credit hours than others are given precedence, no matter how they produce them and regardless of the relative adaptability of different disciplines to large lectures and machine-graded testing—two essentials of high credit-hour production per faculty member.

Quality is lost in the numbers-game competition for quantity as the student-teacher ratio grows. Administrations seek numerical accountability from faculties; legislatures seek financial accountability from administrations; research is discouraged in the face of increased demands for "productive" teaching. Departments that generate more grant money in turn are rewarded with more budget money so that they can generate more grant money. And what degenerates are standards and traditions.

The faddish and modish succeed because they sell well, and each successful gimmick perpetuates its success by locking into a secure, self-serving structure. If the present trends continue, the performing arts will be deported to Bohemia, the study of the fine arts will be dispatched to private drawing rooms and salons, and the humanities will be exiled to museums and saloons. Our campuses will house departments of the practical, the popular, and the applied. Universities will become trade schools, degrees will be bought and sold, and every value will have a number attached to it, with or without a dollar sign.

Sports have not *caused* this continuing process of transvaluation, nor has the process in education corrupted athletics. But both feed upon each other in a mutually destructive symbiosis. It seems to me that the prominence of sports in the eyes and minds of our society is so great that, whatever the first cause may be—and it may be simply a natural human or biological process, if we achieved some reform in athletic practices we could begin a process of raising high the humanistic values again. As educators we should seek the proper tools for teaching. And when it comes to the values we live by, it just may be that sports is the name of the game.

# AFTERWORD

In the fall of 1973, the Capital Bullets, née Chicago Packers a.k.a. Baltimore Bullets and now known as the Washington Bullets, opened their NBA season at Cole Field House on the University of Maryland campus. This was a temporary accommodation, one example of the many ways in which professional sports and institutions of higher education scratch each other's backs—for a price plus future considerations.

Abe Pollin, who had become sole owner of the franchise in 1968, had been trying to bring about a move to the Washington area for some time. But when all projected sites for municipally owned, financed, or assisted arenas met with political or just plain bureaucratic obstacles, the enterprising Mr. Pollin determined to build his own sports palace.

A builder by background, though by profession now a sports entrepreneur—a rarity among the exclusive group of professional sports owners—Abe Pollin set an ambitious timetable for the opening of the Capital Centre. And then he set about meeting his own deadline. Against all odds and all prognostications, battling the problems of supplies and labor disputes and jurisdictional, bureaucratic squabbling, he personally rode herd on this project—in which he had invested his whole life and self, as it were—and the Capital Centre opened on December 2 as he had said it would, for the Bullets versus the Supersonics.

The game sold out, and there was great demand for press credentials. The Bullets, who have always been unfailingly cordial and cooperative to me, had no room at the press table but provided me with a complimentary seat in the ninth row. They were apologetic; I was grateful. I knew there would be a traffic problem so I started out unusually early for the game, but I never anticipated the magnitude of the problem.

The building was ready for play but not finished; the parking lot, however, was not ready, and neither the access roads nor the traffic patterns were anything like adequate. After an inordinate delay even getting off the Beltway, I discovered that the bumper-to-bumper traffic was stalled by the fact that whole lanes of cars were simply pulling up and parking at the side of the access road. It was past game time when I did the same, but my radio told me that the tip-off was being delayed so that the crowd could see the event.

By the time I negotiated the two-mile walk, passing many tired and bitching fans but not matching the time of the few joggers in the crowd, I had indeed missed the tip-off (and the ceremonies—which almost made it worthwhile) but only a few minutes of play. And when I got to my seat I realized how Pollin had been able to open on the announced date, regardless of insuperable delays. He had simply concentrated on the basics and left the unnecessaries to be finished up later.

For one thing, the temporary seats in the first dozen rows, which are removed for hockey, were pretty rickety that opening night. I was a little concerned not only walking down the temporary steps but even sitting in the temporary row. Nevertheless, what bothered me most that night—not the rough-hewn, unfinished appointments, not the hike to the building, not the hours spent getting home later—was missing a few minutes of play.

I confess that I do not like to miss any action in a game. I hate missing kickoffs and faceoffs. I even hate to have to take a halftime piss lest I miss a second-half tip-off (now happily eliminated in the NBA). But most of all—and this is what leads to the point of this personal reminiscence—I hate missing the play at the end of the game.

I am—my chess inexpertise notwithstanding—an endgame fancier. I don't mean just those games where the result is in doubt up to the final buzzer, and I don't mean just those games where the point-spread is in doubt. I also mean, and perhaps I especially mean, those games where no result is in doubt at all.

The play that goes on at such times is intriguing to me. For one thing, you often see players you don't see at any other time. But more important, you see the attitudes of individuals, players, coaches, teams, organizations, and fans as well, toward the game itself. If you are looking for signs of integrity, of both self-respect and community concern, in athletics, these are the times when they can be seen. Where no tangible issues remain in doubt, the intangibles may become apparent without complicating qualifications.

And so I am obsessive/compulsive about watching the ends of games, and I don't really understand people who leave just because the winner is determined, never mind the point-spread. Mostly, though, I don't understand the people who leave when the issue is doubt. Can they come to games knowing so little about them that they don't know what can happen in the endgame? Or can they care enough to come on the one hand but care more about beating the traffic home on the other?

At any rate, I am one who stays for the "garbage game" at the end of basketball routs or the desperation passes and interceptions in one-sided football games. When I next went to the Capital Centre for the Bullets-Pistons game it was 34 days later but little more substantial work had been done on the place during the holidays—in all fairness I must note that it is now one of the finest in the world for watching basketball and hockey. Those temporaries were still (and still made me) a little shaky, but I was back in a choice seat at the press table and delighting in the vantage from which I could observe and analyze what I think is the most interesting of all sports, NBA basketball.

The Bullets were playing well and holding a steady lead well into the second half, Wes Unseld playing one of his best games of the season against Bob Lanier, making it easy for Phil Chenier, Elvin Hayes, and Mike Riordan to get their points. With about eight minutes left to play, they led by 12 points—not anything like a sure lead with the twenty-four-second clock, Clair Bee's greatest gift to the game we love. Suddenly I had a vision. I mean that as literally as I can. A clear image appeared in my mind's eye of the building collapsing. I did not experience fear or anxiety. I did not really "feel" that the roof would fall on me. There was no personal, emotional involvement whatsoever. I saw in a flash, as if from the outside and impersonally, a still shot of the building with the roof caved in.

For some minutes I continued to watch the game, but with increasing frequency I was getting flashes of the collapse, so many pictures that I had in my head what amounted to a series of stop-action shots that presented the "event" in a graphic slow-motion sequence. So strong was the impression that I could not stay. Still without experiencing any anxiety, but unable to select out the compelling images, I walked briskly away from the table and up the aisle toward the exit nearest my car. Some snide comments accompanied me, but I never hesitated.

The Capital Centre did not collapse. I beat the traffic. The Bullets did not collapse; they beat the Pistons 93–90, the margin narrowing only in the final two minutes when the result had been decided.

Next morning on the front page of the *Washington Post* there appeared a sequence of pictures that matched in many particulars the pictures in my mind the night before. The building was the Capital Garage on New York Avenue NW in the District, and it was being demolished by a carefully planned explosion. It was then for the first time that I experience some emotional involvement with the phenomenon, because I couldn't easily explain what had happened, or how I had known (without knowing just what I knew) what was going to happen.

The point of this story is not to demonstrate my prescience. I claim no special powers, though perhaps I may claim to be somewhat more aware of powers of precognition than most. No matter. The experience was sufficiently extraordinary to compel me to do what I could never do under ordinary circumstances. I walked out of an NBA basketball game with about five minutes of play remaining.

The point, then, is a context of values. There are times when I must put my sports fandom in perspective. There are situations in which and conditions under which the fascination with sports in general and sporting events in particular must give way to matters of relatively greater importance.

It now seems to me that the prescient vision I had, albeit mistakenly applied to Abe Pollin's Capital Centre instead of the Capital Garage, was an allegory for this book which I had not at the time decided to write. The sports edifice which our society has erected has both overt and hidden flaws in its construction—in its architecture, its superstructure, its materials, and its appointments. If we do not apply a rigorous code of standards to that construction, and if we do not vigorously and continually inspect for violations of that code, the model we have built in all innocence and admiration, in all complicity and cynicism, in all emotional warmth and rational cool, will either collapse or have to be exploded. In either case, the values that are the foundation of our social system will be crushed or torn down to make way for the cultural renewal or cataclysm to come.

# INDEX